Light From Water
Resurrecting the Teachings of Jesus from Corporate Christianity
Freeing Jesus

Thomas F. Kearns

Copyright © 2018 by Thomas F. Kearns
Copyright © 2019 by Thomas F. Kearns
All rights reserved. This book or any portion thereof
may not be reproduced or used in any manner whatsoever
without the express written permission of the author
except for the use of brief quotations in a book review.

Printed in the United States of America

Cover Art & Manchurch Poster by Frank Herec
Stained Glass Window on Cover by Amy Hayes

First Printing: 2019

ISBN #978-0-935251-01-2

Manchurch Publishing
P. O. Box 4114
Albany, NY 12204

Dedication

To Merlin:
Master of the Old Ways,
and Guardian of Magic.

Saint Harriet:
For the Strength of Her Faith,
the Love in Her Heart,
and the Power of her Determination.

To All Those Children Who Have Come into This World
On a Spiritual Journey. I Have Crossed Paths With Some of You, and
I Have Walked on the Same Path with Others.
All of Our Footsteps Are Woven Together in the
Sacred Tapestry Of Life.

To Those Who Have Been Harmed by Religion, May This
Book Help Heal You and Set You Free.

Painting of Merlin

The stories of Camelot, Merlin, Arthur and Excalibur have captivated me since childhood. My pursuit of Spiritual Development under the guidance of my teacher, the Rev. Harry Bender brought me to Temple Heights Spiritual Camp in Maine in the 1970s. His teachings, and the experiences gained there opened me to new understanding and possibilities. I explained them in my book, *The Art of the Mystic*.

I have traveled to Temple Heights many times to serve the camp and enjoy the people, spiritual experiences, and scenery. I acquired the Merlin sock creature at the Jelly Mill in Manchester, Vermont, on one such journey. It has traveled with me to many destinations ever since. At Temple Heights, I would place Merlin in the window so he could enjoy the view of Penobscot Bay. Nancy Teel, a friend, artist, and volunteer who shared my love for Temple Heights captured Merlin as he gazed off into the distance.

An activity shared by all seekers of mystery.

Oil on Canvas 11 x 14

TABLE OF CONTENTS

THE PROLOGUE - EXPLOITATION	1
Light from Water - A Cosmic Concept	5
A Spirit Wounded	6
CHAPTER 1 - FOUNDATIONS	7
Little Big Things	9
The Teachings of Fear	11
A Christmas Gift	13
Instant Karma	14
The Nun from Hell	16
A Rude Awakening	18
Midtown and Back	19
A Comic Book Hero	21
Oh! The Problem with Sex	22
CHAPTER 2 - A SECONDARY EDUCATION	23
High School	23
Discipline, the Old Fashioned way	25
My First Catholic Bump	26
My Second Catholic Bump	27
My Third Catholic Bump	29
College Chaos	30
CHAPTER 3 - LIFE IN THE REAL WORLD	33
Wedding Bell Blues	33
Work Realities	35
Its All in the Stars	38
Embarrassment and Infuriation	38
Rebirth in Rochester	39
Crushed Again by Love	43
Another Priestly Moment	47
Postgraduate	49

CHAPTER 4 - FREEING JESUS — 51

A Walk With Jesus	51
Lecture on Genesis	54
Commentary on Genesis	61
The Woman Taken in Adultery	63
Jesus on Love	65
Jesus on Divorce	68
Jesus on Hate - The Beatitudes and Woes	69
Money and Christianity	71
Who Did Jesus Hate?	73
The Scribes and Pharisees	75
The Last Supper	76

CHAPTER 5 - FOUR PATHS TO PASSION — 81

Seven Last Words of the Crucified Jesus	84
The Tomb	87
Crucifixion or Resurrection - Prometheus Bound	91
A Few Questions for You to Consider	92
Jesus the Archetype	93
The Body and Blood	93
The Crucifix	94
The Material Route	96
Promises not Kept	97
Jesus on Prayer	97

CHAPTER 6 - THE POWER OF AN IMAGE — 101

The immaculate Conception	102
Saint Harriet	104
WWJD	105

CHAPTER 7 - WHO WILL FREE JESUS? — 107

CHAPTER 8 - MANCHURCH — 111

Thomas F. Kearns

THE PROLOGUE - EXPLOITATION

Jesus is perhaps the most exploited and brutalized figure in the history of the world. No wonder he said, "Father, forgive them; for them know not what they do." (Luke 23:34)[1] Many people see Jesus as love and forgiveness incarnate, the savior of the world. How could the light of the world, be represented by the darkness done in his name throughout history? How could the teachings of love become so twisted? Is it surprising that priests exploited so many children? Is it surprising that so many people died in the name of Jesus? It should be! Christianity has capitalized on the teachings of Jesus by perverting them. The Christian movement created a cultural model of salvation, only they controlled, and only they could provide. They exploited and cornered the market to salvation, and held the faithful hostage to it through propaganda, manipulation, and guilt associated with the suffering of Jesus. However, look closely and honestly, and see the Christian model is the exact model Jesus detested. (If you believe the New Testament.) Jesus was a radical teacher and revolutionary leader. He hated the church bureaucratic. The church bureaucratic, the Scribes and Pharisees, hated him. He threw a shadow upon them and threatened their power. Jesus participated in the temple traditions, but he probably did not go to services every week, he lived his beliefs every day. That is one reason why they killed him.

    The conquerors and military occupiers of the land knew about Jesus. The people of the towns and countryside heard him teaching and preaching. Multitudes heard his message. A Roman Centurion knew about Jesus and went to him for his help. The Roman conquerors would keep an eye on him. An occupying government in a rebellious community keeps tabs on any possible threat of rebellion. Jesus had two enemies, the Jewish church bureaucratic and the Roman oppressors. The followers of Jesus, who would later write the New Testament, were afraid of the power of the Roman occupiers and did not attack them in words or deeds. However, they were not afraid to attack their rivals, the Jewish church bureaucratic.

Christianity is full of rules and regulations that have nothing to do with a personal relationship to God, the way Jesus expressed it. That is what Jesus taught. He did not consider intermediaries (Scribes and Pharisees) to be either helpful or necessary. He said, "Go ye therefore, and teach all nations." Not control all people. (Matthew 28:19) Why all the different churches? How many various Christian organizations and interpretations are there? Why all the priests? Who and what did Jesus attack? Jesus attacked the Pharisees and Scribes. His target: their hypocrisy and legalism. (Matthew 23:1-39, Luke 11:37-54) Would he ever approve of a system that grew more and more bureaucratic, and more and more distant from people? The teachings of Jesus and the Old Testament were used by Christianity to create a God who became the boogie man. He would not only disown you; if you didn't follow the rules, He would also burn you in hell forever. He did drown almost everyone! Christianity has excelled with the twin themes: you can only get to heaven through Jesus, and you can only get to Jesus through Christianity. Unfortunately, they bureaucratized Jesus and codified his wisdom.

I can understand why the Jewish people do not use the word, God, except in prayer. Think of how often you hear the name "Jesus" expressed. Jesus loves you! Jesus died for your sins! The name of Jesus is still used in a sacred manner by many. However, over the ages, his name has become an exclamation and sometimes a curse. The holy name of Jesus, if you believe he is God, should never be used in such a pedestrian manner.

Thomas F. Kearns

Jesus was not a Christian. If he was the Messiah, he was Jewish, not Christian. The teachings of Jesus were new, radical, and different. They were revolutionary. Jesus taught God was love. He explained the experience of heaven was at hand. He taught people to open their hearts to God and others (the greatest commandments). Jesus said, "The time is fulfilled, and the kingdom of God is at hand: repent and believe in the gospel." (Mark 1:15) Heaven is here, and now, God is within us, and all around us. God is present always. His teachings remind me of the core theme in the teachings of Siddhartha Gautama, the Buddha, "to live in the present moment." I was fortunate to study Philosophy with a track in religion, and then teach World Religions as an Adjunct Professor at the University at Albany, SUNY. Studying and teaching helped me understand, there are different "truths."

I once heard a statement by a now tarnished political commentator about Buddhism. He proudly reports, he is a Roman Catholic. Catholics are one-branch, of the many branches of Christianity. They think they are high Christians. I know, I grew up as one of them. He was laughing at the fact Buddhists don't believe in God. That sounds very bad. Before looking at Buddhism to see if this statement is true, I would like to offer a short introduction to Hermann Samuel Reimarus.

Reimarus began the search for the historical Jesus. He lived from 1694 to 1768. He was a professor of Oriental Languages and Hebrew. He was a free thinker and philosopher. Imagine going to a Catholic Church, or another Christian service on Sunday morning. The priest or minister has studied the work *Fragments*[2] which was written by Reimarus but only published after his death. It has shaken him and his faith. He climbs the pulpit stairs heavy in heart. A feeling mirrored by his heavy footsteps. He begins his lecture with a quivering voice. He quotes Reimarus' words "Jesus was a failure." Wow! That would awaken the congregation. He has studied the New Testament in a new light. He goes on to describe some of the failures noted in his newly enlightened study: Jesus did not rise from the dead; he did not save sinners, as promised; the "Son of Man" has not been seen in the clouds of heaven, and the Kingdom has not come. Although the faithful are warned, it could happen at any moment. Be prepared! I doubt the minister would have survived the day! Reimarus was wise to protect himself by hiding his work until after his death. Imagine if the Christians of today got hold of him.

Buddhism is a fascinating religion. The Buddha didn't teach about metaphysical topics such as the purpose of creation, is there a God, and other unknowable theories. If God is infinite, how can a finite human mind ever hope to comprehend and understand God? Only an enlightened being could. The Buddha "The Enlightened One" or "The Awakened One" taught the fundamental nature of life is suffering. Our desires cause it. Just look closely at life, and you may see what the Buddha saw. His primary focus was to understand the process that creates suffering and then do something to stop it. His method is known as: "The Noble Eight Fold Path." Now let us look at the effects of the teachings of the Buddha. I am not a Buddhist. I respect some of the teachings attributed to the Buddha, as I appreciate some of the teachings attributed to Jesus.

There are significant similarities between Jesus and the Buddha. You will find them in the concepts they taught and in their lives. Here are some: Both reportedly had miraculous births. Both started their ministries around the age of thirty. The period around thirty is a vital time called a "Saturn return" in Astrology. Jesus went into the desert. The Buddha went into the forest. They both overcame temptation from the devil. Jesus and Buddha both lived simple lives, owned nothing, taught clarity and love, and had followers. Here is one significant difference. The old saying is, "The proof is in the pudding." Look at the twenty-five hundred-year history of Buddhism. How many people were killed or tortured in the name of the Buddha? I know of none. Was there ever a Buddhist crusade or inquisition? Was there a Buddhist war? Never! Do no harm! An honorable practice. Have you heard of a Buddhist killing people in the name of God? Perhaps there are benefits to not believing in the existence of God, or not being able to understand the essence of God. The Buddhists believe, the path explained by the Buddha works. Now, reflect on this conclusion of Reimarus: Jesus tried to save the world and failed. I add the Buddha wanted to change himself and succeeded. He gave the world a path to salvation. My spirit is torn!

Now let us look at the history of the Religions of the Book. You need to imagine the number of people who have been tortured and killed by followers of religions of the book (Judaism, and Christianity). Use a powerful computer to count them. Each of these religions believes in one true God. God commanded: "Thou shalt not kill." (Exodus 20:13) However, over the centuries, countless people have been victims of religion. Would that make anyone proud? Should anyone laugh at that? Would Jesus be pleased? People kill each other for many reasons. However, it seems only the people who believe in God, are the people who kill and die in the name of God. People who kill or harm in the name of Jesus lay blame at the foot of the cross and on Jesus' shoulders. I respect the teachings of Jesus, as best they can be identified, minus the legalism of the new Scribes and Pharisees (Christian priests, ministers, and theologians). Here is a critical one: "A new commandment I give unto you, That ye love one another; as I have loved you, that ye also love one another." (John 13:34)

LIGHT FROM WATER - A COSMIC CONCEPT

"Light from Water" expresses a simple concept captured in the changing cycles of the ages and the concurrent philosophies of man and womankind. The popular *Aquarius*[3] by the Fifth Dimension captured the movement into the new-age in a song. The words "let the Sunshine in" can be used to express the idea of moving from the emotional Age of Pisces, represented by the element Water, the fishes, and Jesus, to the more intellectual, humane, and peaceful Age of Aquarius. The Olympian Gods mourned the loss of human worship and respect. Perhaps the One God represented by the "Religions of the Book" will now mourn the loss of human-worship, as humanity grows toward an intellectual and scientific understanding of the world "Light or Illumination." But fear not old gods, we will still need you. Man has been the author of our past religious traditions and their positive and negative effects, so man will also be the author of our new illumination. It is a scary thought. Will the human experience change in the future? Past evidence does not bode well for the future. Humankind now has the power of science in its hands. Will we be illuminated? Will there be peace on Earth, or will the power available to man and womankind through science, bring darkness to cover the face of the Earth once more? Our scientists warn us of Global Warming. Ask them, who created the technology responsible for this dangerous condition?

A SPIRIT WOUNDED

To live in this world is to be wounded. The vicissitudes of life can hurt anyone, either on the surface, or deep inside, according to their sensitivity. I hope you understand this fundamental reality. If you do not, watch the news. I am not negative because the beauty and potential in life are also incredible. I am just stating a "factual" opinion. I think the Buddha was correct when he taught "Dukkha" or "the fundamental nature of life is suffering." I am tempted to say; suffering starts when we are born. However, in reality, it all begins before we are born. The people who believe in reincarnation will readily agree we are the product of Karma. I refer to the story of the farmer sowing his seeds in the New Testament, as a representation of the Law of Karma. (Matthew 13) Healthy seeds, on good ground, with good weather, brings the reward of a good crop. Or, in the case of people, a good life with a good experience. Those who don't believe in reincarnation, and think there is a one-allotted lifetime, should refer to the teachings of Jesus, concerning John the Baptist: "And if ye will receive it, this is Elias, which was for to come." (Matthew 11:14) But even if you don't believe in reincarnation, the experience of life and our formation as individuals, still starts before we are born. We all have inherited characteristics and experiential influences that affect us. The traits are easy to comprehend according to the science of DNA. However, it may be more challenging to understand the effects we experience preparing for our journey while in the womb. We know diet, drugs and alcohol abuse, smoking, and other physical factors can affect the fetus. We also know stress, and different emotional experiences may play a role. If the mother-to-be is living in fear or want, the developing being will be affected and very likely wounded. There are a myriad of possibilities in this life for wounds, both unseen and seen.

Thomas F. Kearns

CHAPTER 1 - FOUNDATIONS

My opinions may be different from yours, but I feel what I will address later is quite significant. I believe it will be beneficial for you to understand my developmental experiences. They have affected me emotionally, influenced my thinking, attitudes, and actions in life. I have no sense of being better than anyone. There are few saints among us. We all have a path to follow. We all make mistakes. I hope you can learn from some of mine. In that sense, this is a teaching book, a healing book, and a path to freedom. You are wounded, perhaps worse than I. I can't count the wounds that have attacked my spirit. I don't even know all their origins. Do you? I don't consciously know all of mine, but they began early in life. I was born into an average hard-working family, with roots in Irish and German ancestry. My grandmother, Cunegunda, named after St Kunegunda, came to this country with her father Conrad from Germany. A prosperous and successful architect he crossed the Atlantic many times by steamship. He later moved his family to New York. It was before WW I. Unfortunately after the Great War broke out, and due to anti-German prejudice, he was not first on the list to get a job. He tried his best to support his family and did odd construction jobs. He died by falling off a roof. Cunegunda was a teenager when this occurred.

Grandpa Timmy, named after the first-century Christian bishop of Ephesus, was an Irish immigrant from County Cork. He worked on the Hudson River docks, unloading cargo and luggage from the large ocean crossing steamships. It was mostly the rich who could travel, as the Great Depression was rearing its ugly head. Travel usually lasted weeks to months, not days, and luggage often consisted of several steamer trunks. Grandpa Timmy saw an opportunity and bought a small truck in 1931. He planned to take luggage from the docks to the hotels like the Waldorf Astoria. It was an opportunity to start his own business, York Express. It was in the depths of the Great Depression, and they must have struggled to get by. Both Timmy and Cunegunda shared a strong and conservative Catholic faith. My mother was one of their five children, four of them girls, and a boy, who didn't make it.

Much about my mother's childhood is a mystery to me. She was baptized in St Patrick's Cathedral in Manhattan. She was smart and skipped grades in Catholic School. Rheumatoid Arthritis attacked her in her teen years. She was a beautiful woman with a powerful driving spirit. Despite her disease and its issues, she was popular and able to attract a husband. My mother and her family were industrious. I know little about my father's side of the family. He was born in Cairo, New York in 1920. His family moved to New York City to find work during the depression. My father never had a chance to finish High School, and enlisted in the Marines in World War II. Soon after marrying my mother, he shipped out to San Diego for training. My mother, pregnant with my older sister, followed him there. She had little money and had to sleep on the floor of the lady's room, during the cross country train trip. He served in the Third Marine Aircraft Wing and was a support person during the Okinawa operation. He was paid $228.43 upon his honorable discharge and had attained the rank of Sergeant. Like many after the war, he had few, if any prospects for gainful employment. He wanted to live in the country and become a forest ranger, but out of necessity, he began working on the trucks with my grandfather in Manhattan, a different kind of forest.

It seems there was bad blood between my mother's and father's families, and my mother's side was more dominant. My mother's laments over her difficulties with my father, who became a raging alcoholic, would be met by my grandmother's earthy comment, "You made your bed, now lie in it!" I do remember hearing some stories about my father as a child. He was overactive and would be given beer in his bottle to put him to sleep. His family was poor, and as the story goes, if someone came knocking at the door, his mother would grab him, and the other children and hide in a closet. I can only assume they were hiding from the bill collector. Imagine the effect this had on a child's development. Difficult may not be the correct word to describe the conditions these people lived through. They were weaned on two World Wars and the Great Depression. There was real fear and uncertainty in their lives. It helped form their addictive attachment to religion. You needed a lot of faith to get through each day. The attitudes of fear, poverty, and uncertainty were handed down through the family, and in much of our culture.

LITTLE BIG THINGS

Like many of the baby boomers, this was the atmosphere I inherited at birth. A great deal of uncertainty filled the air, as tremendous social, political, and economic upheaval moved the world. I don't remember much of my early childhood, but I do remember an undercurrent of unhappiness and insecurity present in our family. These feelings became more intense as time moved forward. My mother's condition became more challenging and painful, and my father's drinking, profuse. These conditions left marks of uncertainty on my soul and scars on my heart. We lived in Whitestone, New York, which was a decent area in Queens. I guess we were better off than many other families, but it was always a struggle. I remember my mother crying about money problems, and rushing to the bank whenever a check came in the mail. As an adult, I realized it was fortunate circumstances forced me to be different from the other kids, but growing up, it was a tragedy. Many little things in life become big things that affect us more than we realize. It will probably sound funny, but one of the things that bothered me most as a kid was my nickname "T. J." for Tom Junior. It made me the only kid in the neighborhood, who didn't have a real name like Charlie, Pete, or George, and the kids picked on me because of it. It doesn't sound tragic, but most kids want to fit in and be accepted by the other kids. Kids can be cruel, and if they sensed a weakness or difference, they would taunt you. As a child, you do not know how sensitive you are, and you do not have good personal filters. The name-calling experience would become truly devastating in High School.

I attended St. Luke's Grammar School in Whitestone, New York, from the first through fifth grade. I don't remember much of my grammar school experience. There were too many children in each class, and the nuns would hit you with a ruler if you were causing trouble. I got it more than a few times. And oh, by the way, if you went home and told your mother, you'd get hit again. The nuns or priests couldn't be wrong, like Jesus, they walked on water. You must be guilty! Lawsuits against schools or teachers, no matter how bad they were, didn't exist. I do remember being afraid of going to school on the first day - mother separation. Saint Harriet, my mother, and I will explain this name later, had a potent influence on me. You don't realize how powerful your mother can be, but I was a sensitive little boy, and life at home was difficult at best. I must have overeaten junk food one day, or I had a stomach virus because I felt very sick in school. I went to the principal's office, and my mother was called to pick me up and take me home. While I was waiting, the principal (the top gun nun) told me to go to the bathroom. I followed her instructions, but there was a problem. There were germs in bathrooms. My mother told me so!

My mother would later tell me, "I was the best of her four children." I could makeup games and play by myself for hours and gave her some freedom. It is also the positive side of the power of a vivid imagination. However, it does have its drawbacks. I had never used a bathroom outside my house. I was afraid to sit on the toilet seat - I might get germs! Not that I knew what a germ was. I knew that bathrooms, other than the one at home, and toilet seats, were terrible. I got this insight from my mother. Now, after seeing many public toilets, and the way people dirty them, I can commiserate with my mother's dislike of public bathrooms. It is unfortunate, but young boys and teenagers have this unusual habit of peeing on the seat. I guess they're marking their territory. I remember standing in front of the stall looking in, but I could not use the toilet. The germs must have been monsters. I went back to the principal's office - sat on the hard wooden bench - and had diarrhea in my pants. It was very embarrassing and uncomfortable. I still feel bad for the principal and my poor mother, who had to take me home and clean me up. When she asked me why I hadn't used the bathroom in school, I told her she warned me about the germs in bathrooms. I wonder what she thought about that? There must've been an awful aroma.

Perhaps, I was a little too smart for the level of teaching, or the class size played a factor, but after a few years, I went from winning spelling bees', to getting tossed out of Catholic grammar school by the nuns. I see this as one of my badges of courage. I probably had enough of them, and they had enough of me. It must be challenging to be a nun. They expelled me by the end of the fifth grade. The deteriorating atmosphere at home and my natural energy and enthusiasm caused problems in school. I had also gotten in with the wrong group of boys. Can you imagine that happening in a Catholic School? At home, my father's drinking was worse, and my mother, who was a victim of the intense and unrelenting pain of Rheumatoid Arthritis, as well as my father's abuse, cried a lot. My natural sensitivity, the sense of helplessness caused by my mother's pain, and the fear of my father, added to my deep insecurity. I had no defense and nowhere to hide, except in my imagination and prayer. I prayed a lot. It didn't seem to affect the situation, but I prayed a lot. Here are a few of the experiences I remember vividly. They had a significant effect on my early development.

THE TEACHINGS OF FEAR.

Not only was there enough fear to go around in the world, and in my family situation, fear of God was a bonus. Ah, the nuns, they must have been living the dream. Imagine having upwards of 30 to 40 little kids in a classroom all day long. If you think that was too many? It was! But we were the baby boomers, and the schools were full. The nuns must have been very frustrated. They had to be practically saints, but I don't remember God taught as an all-loving, nurturing, and creative being. I remember an emphasis on original sin and going to purgatory or hell. You were going to suffer forever for the sins you didn't commit, or possibly would commit. There is nothing like being prepared. They made you feel; you had little value. I think the ruler on your knuckles was an excellent way of reinforcing the teachings of pain and suffering. When you were doing wrong, you suffered. Hell was waiting for you and you were going to roast there forever. I don't think I had a chance to understand the normalcy of life. Whatever normal might be? Being a very sensitive and imaginative little boy, I was wide open to the teachings of fear, pain, and suffering. These experiences were reinforced in my world every day. I don't think Jesus would like the treatment children received.

Some painful childhood experiences reinforced my feelings. Here is an example. Our family was invited to visit relatives in Bethlehem, Pennsylvania. I don't remember too much about the trip, but I remember waking up while on the road. The car was swaying side to side. My mother was crying, begging my father, who was very drunk, and very mean when he was drunk, to slow down and let her drive. He was very nasty, and I felt imminent and intense danger. I started yelling at my father, the ex-Marine. Here I was, a little kid, yelling at my father to slow down. This man, when he hit you, almost knocked you out. My yelling increased his drunken anger. He screamed at me and said if I weren't quiet, he'd throw us all out of the car. I think a survival instinct set in, as I was terrified but embolden by my fear. I told my mom to let him throw us out; we'd make it home somehow. He pulled to the side of the road and threw us out of the car. I don't remember why, but he reneged, and let us back into the car. We continued our journey. But I will never forget challenging him and being so scared. I didn't know what was going to happen. I guess being bold, even through my fear, was better than dying in the car. The drive settled down after that, but there was one other incident on that trip.

My sister and I were playing in the basement with our relative's kids. For some reason, I wanted to run away from the house. So I

Thomas F. Kearns

snuck outside, forgetting what was in the yard. My mother's uncle was a butcher, and he raised prize-winning Great Danes. I know the dogs were probably friendly, but they scared me. I tried to hide from them, but they followed me into the bushes growing on the side of the house. They were bigger than I was, and all they did was stand in front of me, probably out of curiosity. And naturally, their big snouts were smelling me. I thought I was going to be dinner.

Writing about this reminds me of a similar situation at the movie theater. Going to a movie was a big-time special treat. I think it was my first time seeing a film on such a large screen. Our TV had a tiny screen. I was still a little kid, and I got terrified. Watch out for that overactive imagination! You'll probably laugh about this, as I do now. Picture yourself as a little kid in a dark movie theater. The movie was about *Rodan*[4] a flying monster. It was a terrible Japanese film. The beast was flying around attacking cities, making a lot of scary noises, and killing people. He was the devil incarnate. Well, I thought for sure, I was dead. In one intense scene, the giant pterodactyl creature was coming straight at us. My imagination went wild, and I thought the monster was actually in the theater. He was going to eat everyone!

I was so terrified, I ran out of the theater and hid, cowering under the marquee, waiting for the monster to come and get me. I only wish they had a PG - 13 ratings for movies back then. My powerful imagination has served me well throughout my adult life, but as a sensitive little boy, it was unnerving. Bedtime could also be scary. I slept in a half-finished attic all alone. On many nights; I pulled the covers over my head because of the people I saw in my room. I'm not the first child to report seeing spirits in a dark room, but I couldn't tell anyone. They wouldn't believe me. The people I was seeing were probably the devil's helpers. Thanks, Catholic Church! In reality, these experiences were quite normal, and a precursor to the psychic and spiritual gifts I would develop as an adult.

A CHRISTMAS GIFT

Here is a funny experience that occurred when I was in grammar school. It must have been around Christmas time, or someone's birthday because my mother was wrapping gifts. You can imagine it was frustrating for a woman with crippled hands to wrap gifts. She had to wrestle with the paper, the scissors, and the tape. It wasn't easy for Saint Harriet. I was very excited and running around like a crazy little boy - guess that's what I was. My mother kept telling me to be quiet and behave, but when a kid is on a high (probably had too much sugar), it's hard to use words to stop him. She was in pain, and it would've been impossible for her to get up and grab me. She did the next best thing. She hit me with the tube of wrapping paper. Most wrapping papers came on a cardboard tube. Unfortunately, she did not know there was a piece of metal at the end of the tube. When she hit me, she hit me in the head. I went down like a rock. She must've scared the hell out of herself because I remember she treated me like a little king for the next few weeks.

INSTANT KARMA

Instant Karma struck me in the fourth or fifth grade. I don't know how the incident started, but as you know, schoolchildren do the pecking order thing. They try posturing to prove themselves, and during the process, they can be quite mean. Perhaps I was mean, or some other boys incited the event. Boys will be boys, and somehow a fight began, or a pushing match started between another boy and me. I remember he was smaller than I was, and partially crippled by polio. He may have had a bit of a chip on his shoulder. He might have been trying to prove himself. A few pushes would have been the end of it, but the bigger boys took note of our posturing and forced a showdown between us after school.

We wound up in a vacant lot down the street from the school. It was half grass and half dirt and blocked off from the road by some hedges. I did not want to fight this boy. I could've easily beat him, and perhaps hurt him. He was crippled, and my mother was crippled. I knew of her pain, as I often heard her crying and struggling. How could I hit someone who was crippled? Name-calling and pushing are one thing, physically hurting someone is another. I did my best to fake a fight with him. I could easily stay away from him, but the bigger boys wanted blood. They told me, if I did not fight harder, they would beat me up bad. Since there were seven or eight of them, I complied. To make the best of a bad situation, rather than punch and kick, I decided to wrestle. Wrestling meant we hit the ground and rolled around in the dirt. The fight lasted long enough to satisfy the older boys, and I allowed the smaller boy to win somewhat. But my blue pants, white shirt, and tie, the infamous Catholic School uniform, got the worst of it. Money was a constant family struggle, and you can imagine when I got home, in a dirty and torn uniform, my mother was not a happy camper.

Remember, in those days, whatever happened, you were wrong, and you were going to pay for being wrong. My mother was furious at me for fighting and just as angry at the ruined school uniform. She decided she was going to give the other boy's mother a piece of her mind. I tried my best to stop her, but she would have none of it. Her mind was made up, and she was going to get satisfaction. I clearly remember she would not listen to me. I tried to explain, I didn't want to hurt the other boy, and that's why I was so dirty and torn up. Polio had crippled him, and you see, my mother was also crippled. How could I hit a crippled person, when I heard my mother crying in pain almost every day? I think part of her disease reflected in her stubbornness and determination. She would not deny her feelings. She grabbed me and her crutches, and off to the boy's house, we drove.

When we arrived, she had to drag me to the front door. She needed evidence. After a few loud knocks, the boy's mother came to the door. My mother started yelling at her, "Look at what your son did to my son. He beat him up and ruined his clothing. How could you let your son be so bad?" The boy's mother said nothing. She just brought her son to the door. Her son was wearing a brace on his crippled leg and using a crutch. When my mother saw the smaller, obviously crippled boy, she was embarrassed into quiet. We sheepishly left the house after my mother apologized. We got back into the car and headed home. I remember quietly asking my mother, through my tears, why she wouldn't believe me about the forced fight? And why she had to do, what she had just done? I had tried to be good, as good as I could be, considering the older boys, but she wouldn't listen to me. My heart and eyes were full of tears.

THE NUN FROM HELL

My mother must have been heartbroken when the nuns threw me out of school in the fifth grade, but she was a trooper and undaunted. Her little boy was not going to public school; he was going to get an excellent Catholic education. She knew how important education was, and I was going to get a good one, whether it killed me or not. Two of my mother's sisters had been in the convent, one left due to illness, and the other became a Sister of Charity. She also had a cousin who was a Sister of Charity, and the eighth-grade teacher in a Catholic School in Manhattan. I was shipped off to her. She was going to test me. My mother wanted to find out what was wrong with me. It turns out, I wasn't too slow, and I didn't have any learning difficulties. It appears the real problem was, I was too smart. The size and scope of the Catholic School classroom were not challenging. You had an overly energetic child, with a curious mind, bored to death in school. The perfect recipe for disaster! Well, I didn't know it, but my trouble was only beginning. They decided, I would travel into Manhattan every day to attend grammar school, where my cousin the nun was the eighth-grade teacher. The travel time was an hour each way by bus and subway. The trip was indeed an adventure for a little boy - just like *Pinocchio*[5]. And here I go again, just like "T. J." (The boy with the funny name.) I would be the outsider in a group of children who had been together for several years.

This Sister of Charity was not a happy being. I know she did not like little boys, especially me. Every time I did something, it wasn't good enough. She would put me down or insult my work. I think she enjoyed doing it in front of my classmates. How embarrassing and crushing that can be! There were some terrible moments. The first occurred during a Christmas pageant practice. My voice was pretty good. Whenever the family got together for Thanksgiving or Christmas, I would have to sing the hymns. However, I was also at an age when things were changing. I was chosen to sing Silent Night in

Thomas F. Kearns

the Christmas pageant, while my classmates enacted the birth scene at Bethlehem. During one of our practice sessions, as I was singing the high notes, my voice cracked a bit. Pretty normal during growth changes. Unfortunately, this did not please my cousin the nun. Her pageant had to be perfect. It was going to be in the church. She scolded me in front of my classmates and threw me out of the pageant. When I see the ten and 12-year-old kids, who sing on talent shows, and have their family members supporting them, I feel very happy for them, but my heart still cries.

Another event happened during our recess program. The school was located on East 44th Street between Lexington and Third Avenues. Most of the students were from the East Side. Many of their families came from around the world. The school was the closest Catholic Elementary School to the United Nations. East 44th Street is not a through street in this location. The Grand Central Post Office forces it to end at Lexington Avenue. The police would close it to traffic every once in a while, and we got to do our lunch recess out in the street. When we couldn't use the street, we played dodge-ball on the roof.

The school building was six stories high with a flat fenced-in roof. The game is pretty simple. There are two equal sides. Let's say two teams of 20. There is a semi-hard large rubber ball like a soccer ball. The object of the game is to knock an opposing team member out. You must hit one of the rival team members with the ball on the fly, to do so. If they catch the ball you threw, you were out. As you can imagine, sixth, seventh, and eighth-graders, can be quite competitive. The older boys can throw the ball pretty hard, and there are substantial ego investments involved, based on who wins and who loses. Pride, prestige, and bragging rights are up for grabs. It was during one such game, my cousin the unhappy nun struck again. The teams were matched equally, and all was going well. It came down to myself versus one of the older and bigger boys. I threw my shot low and at his legs because if he caught the ball, I'd lose. He jumped over it. Now it was his turn. He ran up to throwing line, and let the ball fly as hard as he could. The ball came right towards my middle, and I caught it by

17

folding my arms and legs around it in a cradle. My teammates went wild with joy, and I was the hero. Then she struck. She blew her loud whistle and called me out because I had used my legs to help catch the ball. The other team won. She shocked my team! They started to boo. She crushed me! A great win was snatched away by the whim of an unhappy nun. Yes, she got me several times. The singing incident was a blow to the ego, as was the dodge-ball event, made worse because they happened in front of my classmates. However, the deepest wound occurred when she berated my writing. Thankfully, it occurred in private.

I was now in eighth grade, and she was the eighth-grade teacher. Our assignment was to write a creative story, on any subject we chose. I chose to write a space/science fiction story. I loved science fiction. To me, it was an imaginative and exciting story, and I couldn't wait for the praise, and the big A+ grade I would see on the top of my story. She brought me into her office, threw my paper on her desk, and said, "Too bad young man, your story was stupid. I gave you an F!" She had crushed me again.

In case you think I'm hard on this poor woman, listen to this. Many years later, I was visiting my aunt, the other nun in the family, at her apartment in Bronxville. I don't like picking on nuns, because I think there are many good ones, and I believe it can be very difficult to be a nun. I've also had a great friendship with Jun-Sun, a Buddhist nun for many years. While I was having lunch with my aunt, the nun, lo and behold the phone rang. It was my cousin, the nun, my eighth-grade teacher. She was quite a bit older at this point, and after speaking with my aunt for a while, my aunt said to her, "You'll never guess who's here, little T. J." Although, I was not little anymore. As she said my name, she handed me the phone. I put it to my ear just in time to hear a cruel and unkind voice say, "Put the little monster on." She didn't know I had heard her, but it explained a lot to me. Too bad she didn't like little boys, and especially me.

A RUDE AWAKENING

My grammar school stories would not be complete without the

following two events. They both happened in the 11 to 13 year age range. The first was with little Bobby. He was part of our Boy Scout group at a local church. He wanted me to camp out with him on a sleepover in his backyard. It was going to be a test run, for we were going to go camping with the Boy Scouts later that summer. He lived a few blocks away, and my mother allowed me to go. We set up a tent and sleeping bags. Finally, it was dark, and we are ready to go to bed. I crawled into my sleeping bag, talking about our upcoming Boy Scout camping adventure. He said he had a great idea, "Let's play, boys and girls. You be the girl, and I'll be the boy."

I didn't understand what he meant. He was fast and before I knew it, he was in my sleeping bag and had my pajamas pulled down. I was lying on my stomach and made an easy target. He tried to put his penis into my behind. I was terribly afraid. I didn't even know what he was trying to do. In those days, we didn't know anything about sex, at least I didn't. There was no sex education, and we certainly never knew anything about rape or homosexuality. All these things were taboo. You couldn't even talk about it. Remember, to the Catholics, even thinking about sex was a sin. I was scared, I was hurt, and I felt powerless. I was crying and didn't know what to do. I went limp, and thankfully, he did too. I guess he was not boy enough to do it, and thankfully, I had kept my legs and buttocks closed just tight enough, just long enough. However, the feeling of violation would not go away. I couldn't tell anyone about this experience. I'd be too embarrassed to tell my mother, and well, my father was just unavailable.

MIDTOWN AND BACK

Grammar school became quite the trip, especially traveling to and fro. Whitestone is about 12 miles from Midtown Manhattan. If you drove it in rush hour, it might take an hour to an hour and a half. If it was raining, 2 hours, and snowing, forget it! So the bus and subway it was, and a 45 to 60-minute commute to grammar school and home. It was an adventure every day, but not always a good one. I was very active and energetic. I would run to the bus stop, and then run to catch the subway train. Oh, if only I had that energy now. I took the number 7 line from Flushing to Grand Central Station. It's the one that runs past Shea Stadium, the Arthur Ashe Tennis Stadium, and the site of the 1964 World's Fair. You might remember seeing the World's Fair buildings in the movie, *Men in Black*[6]. I met one of them, and I don't mean the stars of the film.

One day returning from school, I stood at the front window of the number 7 first car. The number 7 is both a subway and an elevated line. The adventurous part of the trip was standing at the front window, watching the world approach at what seemed to be immeasurable speed. It was like flying through space (There's that vivid imagination again). Sometimes traveling through the tunnels, was as exciting as the trip above ground. Since the front window was prime real estate, you often had to share it with other riders who also knew the adventure of the ride. It was not surprising to have someone stand next to you or behind you. The movement of the subway car swaying back and forth, and bumping forward and back, brought body contact from the other adventurers, but rarely touching contact.

You can imagine my great shock, and the incredible fear I felt when a man was standing too close to me at the window. I remember he was wearing a raincoat, and he smelled. His upper body pushed against me, so I could not move, and I felt his hand rub up and down inside my buttocks. He tried to slip his hand up around me so that he could touch my genitals. I can still feel his hot smelly breath on the side of my face. He whispered he'd pay me $10 to get off at the next stop with him. There was a quiet bathroom there, and he would make me feel really good. I guess he thought $10 would be a lot of money to a kid, and he didn't want to fail. It seemed he was touching me forever, and I was too small to do anything about it. But the train lurched one more time, and I broke free. In those days, you could run from car to car, and I did. I wound up in the last car and hid in the corner crying until we reached Flushing, the end of the line. The train stopped, and as soon as the doors opened, I flew out of there like a bird breaking out of its cage. It was a pretty scary experience, and again, I couldn't tell anyone about it.

Thomas F. Kearns

A COMIC BOOK HERO

There was another incident at the end of grammar school, that had a profound impact on my self-esteem. At this stage, young bodies go through significant changes. I have a photo of my younger brother and myself standing on our front lawn. I looked tall and very skinny. I think my hormones didn't like the picture, because suddenly, I was taller and a lot bigger around. But when you grow up on Marvel comic books, cowboys and Indians on TV, and perfect heroes in the movies, that's what you want to look like and be. Like most boys my age, I was doing push-ups, sit-ups, and lifting weights to build up my body. Unfortunately, my genetics were winning, and I was getting bigger all around. Now, I don't mean fat, but bigger. My fight against what would be a more substantial frame would be a lost cause, but I didn't know that. I continued working out as much as I could. The 50 push-ups and sit-ups soon grew to the hundreds. I was doing all this without any knowledge or training. My father was never around, and he probably wouldn't have cared anyway. One day, the excessive amount of sit-ups took their toll. I felt something move in my body. It was a very odd sensation. There was no pain, just a funny movement. When I inspected my stomach area, I found red marks on both sides. Not knowing what they were, and if they represented something terrible, I ran downstairs to my mom and told her what had happened.

I must have caught her on an awful day. When I showed her the marks, she blurted out with cruelty in her voice, "Ha! Those are stretch marks! Now you know what it's like to be a woman!" Boy, I can only imagine how much my mom must've hated her body. At that point, she had given birth to four children, had a miscarriage, and Rheumatoid Arthritis had crippled her. I can understand her feelings now. But at the time, her comment, and the way she said it, had a devastating effect. I was scared and embarrassed. No superhero wanna-be could ever become a hero if he was just like a woman, and especially if he had stretch mark scars on his body. I don't think I ever took my T-shirt off in public, at the beach or anywhere else until I was well into my late 20s. Talk about a loss of self-esteem.

OH! THE PROBLEM WITH SEX

We knew nothing about sex. It was a genuinely taboo subject. All we knew is it was a sin. That included everything from masturbation to fornication. The only type of sex education I received as a boy, were the stories I heard from others, and whatever pictures we could see in Playboy magazine. Fortunately, or unfortunately, the girl-next-door did not suffer from my Catholic propaganda. She was blooming. She knew she had breasts, and she wanted to learn how to use them. I was the closest thing to an experiment, she could find. It was summer, and we would meet in her backyard. She would show me her breasts, and have me caress them. I was more than happy to comply! It was dangerous to do outside, so she told me to come to her window at night. Where again, she would expose her breasts, and have me caress them. Of course, all good things must come to an end. Her father caught us in the act. I say us, but I should have said "me" because it was all blamed on me. She didn't have anything to do with it, because there was that "women are pure" thing. It was always the boy's fault. And unfortunately, that is still one of the false myths of our culture.

CHAPTER 2 - A SECONDARY EDUCATION

HIGH SCHOOL

The first year of High School was traumatic, mainly due to the chaos at home. I barely remember it. I had a hard time fitting in. I didn't have too many friends or connections. I had been in Manhattan for the last three years and didn't go to grammar school with the other kids. I was again, the odd one out. I didn't do too well, but my mother, Saint Harriet, was not going to let the chaos of our family tragedy get in the way of her son's education. She was a determined lady. I think this might have had something to do with her arthritis - fixed body, determined mind. I was going to get a college education, whether I wanted it or not. The funny thing is, I don't think she believed I could get into college. I was shipped off to a Catholic military high school that specialized in college preparation for teenage boys. I don't know how my mother ever paid for it, but education was the prime directive, and she was Saint Harriet.

Cardinal Farley Military Academy was a military boarding school run by the Irish Christian Brothers. It was built on a hill overlooking the Hudson River in Rhinecliff, New York. As I look back, it was a beautiful place, but it was a world away from New York City, my home, and my family. I remember how abandoned I felt after my mother left me on the first day. It was a college preparatory school where military discipline met Catholic dogmatism. The Irish Christian

Brothers had a high success rate getting kids into Catholic colleges. Well, here I was again, the odd man out! I had no friends, no one from my neighborhood attended the school or any other type of connection. I started in my sophomore year, so most of the boys had already bonded in their groups and friendships. Between educational demands, military training, and extracurricular activities, the brothers knew how to keep boys busy and out of trouble. But boys will be boys, and posturing began.

There was a small commissary store where you could buy candy, soda, and cigarettes. Yes, they sold cigarettes. Those were the days! There was a smoking area outside the store, where the guys hung out. The first week wasn't too bad, as the kids were pretty open, but there are always some troublemakers. When you're the new person, you don't fit in, and you become a target. I knew this experience. I was over-sensitized by being called "T. J." (the only kid in the neighborhood without a real name). That was nothing compared to the viciousness I would experience over the next three years. Two of the kids knew each other from Brooklyn. They had been friends before their freshman year, and they were protective of each other. Somehow we got into a disagreement, and I became the target of their wrath. One was very heavy. He didn't have a well-defined neck. His nickname was "no-neck" so original. Nicknames are funny things; some are complimentary and almost heroic; some are destructive. Think of the feelings associated with "gunner" or "the crusher." We had a boy called "Gator" because he had a lot of pimples. His name was heroic because he was a great basketball player.

No-neck and I were arguing when his buddy stepped in to protect him. A very admirable thing to do. However, to protect him, he attacked me. He said I looked like a pig. I do have a bit of an Irish pug nose. That nickname would hang around my neck and drown me for the next three years. Let me tell you; the boys tortured me with it. Many times, they taunted me by singing the song "Would you like to swing on a star . . . Or would you rather be a pig!" Not many of the boys had a nickname like that; most nicknames were cool. It was tough to be called "you pig" or "piggy" all the time, and they knew how to rub it in. It was bullying at its finest. I had to live with that bullying everyday for three years. There was no escape.

DISCIPLINE - THE OLD FASHIONED WAY

My Junior year was a bit better. I guess I got used to the bullying. I still had an outgoing, energetic personality, and it did get me in trouble on occasion. I remember fooling around in geometry class and the teacher saying, "Kearns, you get ten demerits!" The problem was he held up one hand and displayed only five fingers. He was a math teacher, and I laughed. The class followed, and I got a lot more than ten demerits. I wound up marching the parade ground, in full dress uniform carrying a rifle for a few hours. That was not fun. However, it was a lot better than some of the other disciplinary actions the brothers would apply. Most of the teaching brothers were in their mid-20s to 30s, some just out of college. And some of them did not belong in a classroom or locker room with young boys. One was particularly nasty and enjoyed applying corporal punishment. However, the way he did it was not only immoral but illegal. In today's world, he would be in jail for child abuse. The brothers had a little faculty club and pool hall where they would go after dinner each night. It also had a bar. You could tell by the erratic walk and alcohol smell, as they came back to their rooms. I had experienced this type of behavior with my father. If you had done something really against the rules, you would be invited to one of the brother's rooms, to receive the punishment for your actions. In this case, with this brutal man, the penalty was a vicious whiplash with a leather strap. It measured about 36 inches long, by 3 inches wide, and probably 1/4 inch thick.

Well, I must have made the grade, because I got the 9:00 P.M. invitation one night. I don't remember what I did; it's blacked out of my memory. You'll understand why. Just like in military barracks, lights out was at 9:00 P.M. If you were going for discipline, you'd be called down to the brother's room just after lights out. I had never had this experience, so I was scared as I walked down the hall. I entered his room and saw him seated in a large reclining chair. I couldn't see his face, because there was a pole light pointed at me. I felt like I was going to an interrogation in a bad detective movie. He told me I was getting punished for what I had done. He told me to turn around, take down my pajama bottoms, bend over, and hold onto the chair in front of me. When I did, he saw that I was wearing underwear. He became furious, and he said, "Oh no! No underwear! Pull them down!" He had an agenda. I complied and bent over again, although, it felt weird.

There I was, naked and bent over, for this man to feast his eyes on my behind. He stared at me for quite a while. I could hear his clothing rustling, and it sounded like he was licking his chops. I had to listen to him salivating! When I made no move, and he had seen enough or felt guilty or excited enough, he got up from the chair, took two long strides, and hit me as hard as he could. He used his motion and arm strength to brand me across my naked behind. He was an athletic man, a coach. He knocked me, and the chair to the ground. This man not only brutally hurt and embarrassed me; he also violated me. I could not sit down for a few days, and I had a bloody welt across my behind. Of course, he had his jollies, at the cost of any dignity, I might have had left. The experience left not only the scars on my behind but also my emotions and consciousness. And again, I had no one to talk to and no place to go for emotional support. And the other boys, they enjoyed my pain.

MY FIRST CATHOLIC BUMP

Latin was never my favorite subject, but we had to suffer through three years of it. I remember, I even had to make up a semester in summer school. Our Latin teacher was not a nice man. Some people can inspire you to learn. Some people try to teach through intimidation and fear. We had a great trigonometry teacher. He ran across the front of the classroom and jumped up on the desktop to introduced himself. He knew how to inspire teenage boys. The Latin teacher's personality was a mixture of arrogance, cruelty, and cunning. He would quietly sneak around the room, between the rows of cadets with a pointing stick in his hand. If you were doing something wrong or made a mistake in conjugation, you would feel the stick. I must have gotten something wrong, laughed at the wrong moment, or done something else to annoy him. He came up behind me and gave me a full roundhouse to the back of my head. I saw stars! What this evil little man had done, was turn his college ring around into the palm of his hand, and hit me as hard as he could. That bump is still on the back of my head. I hate Latin to this day!

MY SECOND CATHOLIC BUMP

I was now a senior at Cardinal Farley. Seniors had more responsibility and more respect. Not only were we the upperclassmen, but many of us had gained rank. We were now a part of the military establishment. I think I made the rank of Platoon Sergeant. As seniors, we got to live in the senior dorm, which was a separate building. However, there was a problem. There were too many seniors and not enough rooms. Rather than making some decent living arrangements, they just stacked us higher. The rooms were designed to house four cadets. It would be close enough with four young men stacked in a 20 by 20-foot room, but now there were five. I was the fifth person in the room. I had to sleep on an iron spring cot in the middle of the room. As you can imagine, in these close quarters, there was no privacy. It was easy to get on one another's nerves, and for tempers to flare.

The school had a rotating laundry system. You would have to sort your laundry and prepare it for processing. Most of the sorting would happen on a table in the middle of the room. However, one day, one of my roommates decided to sort his dirty laundry on my bed. Can you imagine a teenage boy's dirty and smelly laundry on your bed pillow? Unfortunately, this led to some name-calling and anger which erupted into flying fists. I didn't throw any punches, but he did. Before I could protect myself, he had punched me in the face several times. He was a tough kid from the Bronx, and his punches were effective. He broke my nose and loosened several teeth. That would prove to be a costly proposition. Later in life, a number of my teeth died, and I had to have thousands of dollars worth of dental work. Nothing ever happened to that young man who hit me. In today's world, he probably would've been charged with assault, and been expelled from school. The good old Irish Christian Brothers didn't even take notice. I guess "boys will be boys."

There was a positive side to Cardinal Farley Military Academy. It was a sense of structure, discipline, and security. I can see it as I look back through the chaos of my college years, and the rapid decline of my father. If I had been at home during high school, under the prevailing conditions, I probably would have self-destructed in some way, shape, or form. My father was often drunk on the floor, and when at his best, away in a rehabilitation center. They probably did their best to help him, but he passed into spirit on April 24, 1970. He was a victim of his own chaotic life. He was brought up during the depression; served in the Pacific in WWII; worked at a job he didn't like; had four children to support; and a wife who was in pain every day. Alcohol and cigarettes were there to sooth his scars and pain. He was a victim of unhappiness, and he became a lost soul. Imagine, he wanted to be a forest ranger and wound up being a truck driver in New York City instead. He died the year before I graduated from college; he was 49 years old.

College is supposed to be a fun time. Remember, my mother didn't think I'd even get into college, but I did. Here I was with a chaotic family life, not knowing if my father was going to be sober enough to go to work, or if I would have to cover for him. I had been riding on the trucks, helping out since grammar school, but now I had to do my father's job. I would go to school for a few hours a day and have to come home and go to work. Or, I would work a few hours in the morning, then go to classes in the afternoon. It wasn't a comfortable or productive schedule. What made things worse, I now had some freedom. I was no longer locked away in military school. I had a lot of pent up emotions, and wild oats to sow. To shorten a long story, it took a few extra years and a few different schools, but I finally got my Bachelor's Degree. It was in Psychology with a minor in Education. Well, I guess the real knowledge I received was in survival. I remember when things were especially bad, and prayer didn't help at all, I would go back to yelling at God. The funny thing was he/she didn't seem to notice. My anger proved to be as ineffective, as my prayers.

Thomas F. Kearns

MY THIRD CATHOLIC BUMP

I think God did get a little mad at me because I received my third Catholic bump about this time. The lump is still on my forehead above my left eye. It occurred one morning while I was driving out to Long Island to visit my aunt. I was on the entrance ramp to the Cross Island Parkway. My mother was also entering the highway two cars behind. I don't remember why we were taking two different vehicles, but there must've been a reason. Cross Island Parkway has very short on-ramps. It's difficult to see the traffic coming around the bend. You have to be very careful about entering the flow. Besides, on that morning, two motorcycle cops were sitting at the top of the ramp. They were in a stakeout waiting for speeders. I was going to be very careful about entering the highway. I pulled up to the stop sign, saw traffic coming, and stopped. I had to pull up a bit more, to see the highway traffic coming around the bend towards us. At that moment, the world exploded! My car was rear-ended. My head smashed the steering wheel. My little brother, who was riding with me, bounced around the inside of the car like a soccer ball. It was before seat belts. Little did I know the hand of God had struck my car. A Catholic priest rear-ended me. (Not the first time this happened!)

The smoke cleared, as the two cops pulled us out of the car, My mother was also on the scene. She had witnessed the accident. Had the accident happened today, my brother and I would have been transported by ambulance to the nearest hospital. We'd been the victims of a traumatic event. My mother, who witnessed the near-death of her two sons, realized we were going to live. We were bruised, but we would live. My car got hit in the rear, so it could still be driven. However, the priest's car had hit mine so hard; it could not. My good Catholic mother, Saint Harriet, who lived in fear of God and subservience to the Church and clergy, knowing this man had almost killed her two sons, offered him a ride to the next Church he was serving. The cops should have arrested him for driving while impaired. Of course, they didn't do that in those days, and to an indoctrinated woman, (and probably two Irish Catholic motorcycle cops) a priest could do no wrong. I again gained a subtle but valuable lesson. It seems it was a recurring theme in my life. The Church was valued more than the people. I wonder what Jesus would have thought about that? Jesus gave his life for the people, not for the Church.

COLLEGE CHAOS

College came after high school and along with it, freedom and a bit more chaos. The problem with college was getting admitted. The Vietnam War draft loomed heavy over everyone's head. College was one way to get out of the draft, or at least defer it for a while. There was a lot of competition to get accepted. I was fortunate to get a draft number in the 320s. Saint Harriet didn't think I had much of a chance to get into a good Catholic College. I had to take the SATs a few times, got excellent grades in them, but she probably didn't think, I did good enough. Her lack of faith was understandable because conditions had severely deteriorated at home. She was living a tough life. However, she kept on pushing. One of the reasons I refer to her as Saint Harriet. I had to work on the trucks every day because my father was missing in action, or he couldn't get out of bed because he was drunk. She had me apply to 10 colleges. Imagine her surprise when I got into nine out of ten. They included schools like Notre Dame, Pratt Institute and Fordham University. The only school where I was wait-listed was St. John's University. St John's was the party school. Many students wanted to go there. I went to Fordham, but that didn't work out too well. The three years at Cardinal Farley had been like a prison sentence. Now, I had the freedom afforded by a car, and no one was forcing me to go to class. I had a lot of fun, but it only lasted a year. I don't blame myself too much because of the pain and chaos at home. I remember one particularly difficult night. I went to the park under the Whitestone Bridge. It's a pretty place for being in New York City. The bridge reflects on the water at night. Things were so bad at home; I just needed to escape. I stood on the small sandy beach looking up at the sky. I remember crying, raising my fist, and cursing God. How could God, this all-loving God, who I had prayed to so fervently, allow so much destruction, pain, and sorrow in my family?

The next few years were blurs. It took three schools, but I finally graduated from Mercy College in Dobbs Ferry, NY, with a BS degree in Psychology. I needed that! It probably helped me cope, and make a little sense out of my experiences. I was not interested in behaviorism, but I was particularly attracted to the work of Carl Jung. His work had a spiritual context, and it fit well with my growing interest in Astrology and symbolism. Despite his follower's denials, he used birth charts to understand some of his patients better. I even received decent grades. I'm kind of amazed, since I was working two jobs, and going to school at the same time. I would work in the morning and attend classes in the afternoon and evening. I also worked on the weekends when necessary, and worked Friday and Saturday nights at a college disco on Long Island. There wasn't much time or hope for love and romance. I was lonely and hurting. There was a background feeling of learned unworthiness. Life did not prepare me for this important experience. All the pain and insecurity made things difficult, and there was all that Catholic indoctrination, which didn't seem to fit the real world. Love does have a way of showing up, especially when unexpected.

Light from Water

Thomas F. Kearns

CHAPTER 3 - LIFE IN THE REAL WORLD

WEDDING BELL BLUES
A new social world was opening. A classmate was the manager of a college disco. He wanted me to work on the weekends as an assistant manager/bartender. Up to this time, I had no steady girlfriend. That was about to change. One night I was at the door checking ids when my future wife appeared. She had a week to go before turning 18 and was heartbroken she couldn't get in because of her age. Her birthday was only a few days away. She borrowed a girlfriend's id and got in. She was grateful, and our relationship began. We dated for over two years, and I asked her to marry me. Unfortunately, we were two wounded souls, seeking release and relief from unhappy homes. Both of her parents were alcoholics. She once confided in me, she and her older sister would sit on the attic stairs at night, listening to their parent's fight over sex. He wanted, she didn't. The old Genesis curse from God. I wish I had been wise enough to see a red flag because the same condition flowed into our marriage. It led to years of frustration, divorce, and once again, pain.

    A marriage proposal and all the future planning are supposed to be an exciting and happy time. However, in our case, the challenges were beginning. My mother, Saint Harriet, wanted a large church wedding and reception. We wanted a small garden wedding. Sparks flew, and my mother came to her parent's house, eyes blazing! She tried to work out the details, her way, but it didn't go too well. I remember my mother saying, "You can't have a garden wedding; my friends won't have a place to dance." It all became quite a mess. Trying to be wise, and knowing neither side was going to be happy, we decided to have a small ceremony at her Church (Episcopal – not Catholic) and go on a honeymoon. We wanted to go to the Canadian Rockies. We would drive across Canada to Saskatoon, Saskatchewan, where her sister was attending college and living with her boyfriend. Then our plan was to fly to Calgary, and drive to Lake Louise.

It was a fantastic journey, but it brought to light some of our differences, especially the intimate ones. The Canadian Rockies, Lake Louise, Banff, and Jasper were beautiful. It was mid-September. We drove from Calgary into the mountains. I remember my wife saying, "Look at those clouds, they're so beautiful." I replied, "They're not clouds." She immediately said, "If they're not clouds, what are they?" I replied, "Those are the mountains." They were magnificent. Each morning brought pristine snow to the mountain tops. We even had a night in a private log cabin with a fireplace. It was on the river, and very romantic. The views were spectacular and the hotels exceptional, especially the Banff Springs Hotel and the Chateau Lake Louise. Like all honeymoons, the time was short, and a return to everyday reality and some shocking developments were just around the corner.

I knew my mother was not happy with the marriage situation. However, I thought she would still need me in the family business, as my father was no longer around. Boy was I wrong! I walked into our family home to find her sitting in the kitchen. It was the center where she ran the family business. I looked at her and said, "I know you're not happy with the wedding, but if you need me, I am willing to come back to work." She stared at me with deep hurt and anger in her eyes, and replied, "That's okay son, we don't need you anymore." What a wedding present! I was fired from the business and banished from my family. I would not see Saint Harriet or my siblings again for many years.

Thomas F. Kearns

WORK REALITIES

The next few years were bumpy both in our marriage and at work. I got a job climbing and pruning trees from a friend of my wife's father. It lasted until I fell out of a tree. The manager liked me and trained me to sell their services. The Bartlett Tree Expert Company was an excellent company. They taught me sales and the biological science behind the business. They moved us to Northern New Jersey. Everything was exciting. It was a new start. However, I had to work in a problematic area. The prior manager for the company had been very successful, but he was unhappy with some of the new company regulations. He started a tree service of his own and took all the clients, he had known and serviced for over 20 years with him. My job was a failure, just waiting to happen. It was in the very lucrative Morristown, Bedminster, Chatham, and Benardsville area. Following his act was difficult, but there was also a hidden problem. I had to share an office with a man who covered the adjoining counties. He saw me as competition, and perhaps his replacement. He was covering the business left over from the prior manager, making extra money doing it, and he did not want me in the picture. He saw me as a threat and would do little to help me.

I found this disturbing since he was a part-time Christian minister. He even carried a Bible in his hands all day long. You would think he would have been kind and helpful, but he turned out to be quite the serpent. I have since encountered other born again Christians who have had a similar approach. Don't let their Bible fool you! In my experience, they carried it because they were full of fear. A man full of fear and religion has a steep road to travel. They smile at your face, as they stick a knife in your back. My mother came under the influence of born again Christians when she was at the weakest point in her life. They broke her spirit, and perverted her heart, turning her against her children. As cynical as that is, it is somewhat understandable. Christianity teaches us to hate our parents and families

The Tree Expert job didn't last long, so my next career position was selling outdoor advertising for a company in the same area. I thought I had found my niche. My boss was a nice man who supported me and treated me with kindness. We developed a pretty close relationship, and he would even take my wife and me out to dinner. Some friendships turn bad, and this one would. He promoted me, and the company moved us to Jamestown, New York. I was going to manage a small company they had in New York's Southern Tier.

Jamestown was interesting. It's a small, almost forgotten city with a population of forty thousand people. Jamestown is at the Western end of New York State, South of Buffalo. It was, for two people from New York City, "the boonies." I performed pretty well on the job front, revitalize a dying company. But again, I ran into a Bible carrying employee. He turned out much like the first, and I found I needed to be wary of him. He saw me as a threat to his success, and his Christian ministry did not include kindness to me. He tried to subvert me whenever he could. Oh well, it didn't matter too much, I didn't like Christians, and especially born-again Christians, at this point in my life.

Taking two city people, out of the city, and moving them into a small community, did not work well. My wife could not handle it. She never tried to assimilate or get a job. She isolated herself by staying at home every day. Her most important activity was watching soap operas. After a year of that unhealthy diet, she put her soap opera into motion. I did love her, but we never had a good intimate relationship. It became a vast chasm between us. A particular necessary glue was missing. One morning I woke up before her and began touching her very gently. She became very excited, dropped her defenses, and we made love like we never had before. It was the first time she had opened herself to me. I enjoyed the experience, but it was the last straw for her. Within two weeks, she told me she was leaving, because she couldn't stand Jamestown, and didn't love me. She was cruel and brutal, but more damage was to come.

I did not know it, but she had been corresponding with my former boss back in New Jersey. One night she told me her girlfriend was flying up to Bradford, Pennsylvania to meet her. They planned to drive back to Long Island together. Well, if I had any hope for the relationship to survive, it was destroyed. I tried to change her mind, to no avail. The night she was supposed to go to Bradford, the airport closed due to icing. I was relieved, but she said her friend was going to drive up and meet her there. However, there was a little problem. She did not know how to get to Bradford, and she was afraid to drive in the bad weather. This good-natured guy, who was still in love with her, offered to drive her to meet her friend. She wasn't happy about the idea, but it was her only way out.

The airport was over an hour away. She insisted I was to drive to the terminal, drop her off, and leave. However, when we got to the airport, the weather was so bad, I insisted on waiting until her friend arrived. Boy, I was in for a surprise! It was not her girlfriend who drove in, but my former boss from New Jersey. I kept my temper because I still did not realize the depth of the deception. He had left his wife and two children. They were planning to move in together. Beyond the hurt of that experience, there was another unusual occurrence. We talked for a while, and he tried to put all the blame for my wife's unhappiness on me. Luckily, I disagreed. I finally said to him, "I'm not running away with your wife; you're running away with mine." And then, I made what was to be my first Psychic and Spiritual prediction. I said, "This relationship will not last more than 30 days." Sure enough, they separated precisely 30 days later.

A few months had passed, and we had not begun our divorce. I had to go to Long Island, and I wanted to see my not yet ex-wife. I was still very much in love with her. I wanted to try to heal our relationship. I contacted her, and she agreed to see me. She was living at her parents. It was adjacent to a beautiful park, Old Westbury Gardens. We took a long walk through the gardens and stopped at a particularly idyllic spot under a flowering tree. I gently held her hands, looked directly in her eyes, and said, "I love you, and would be very happy if we could get back together." I guess this pushed her way past her comfort zone, and she said in a rather cruel voice, "I never loved you! I just married you to get away from my mother." I was devastated, and my consciousness was almost out of my body. I slowly pulled her sword from deep within my heart, and I heard myself say, "You can't say that to me, I've kissed you!" I know spirit brought those words to me because I was too destroyed to think. She screamed, burst into tears, and ran away. The point of her sword was deep within my heart. A part of it is still lodged there today, and the burden of its scar has blocked me from opening myself to a truly satisfying relationship. It set a pattern for more unhappiness in the future.

ITS ALL IN THE STARS

As a short addendum to this story, I had to go to Olean, New York, two weeks after the airport incident. I was early for an appointment, so I stopped in a small newspaper store. As I browsed around, I found a yearly Astrology prediction book by *Sidney Omar*[7]. In it were weekly and monthly predictions for my sign, Sagittarius. I had a passing interest in Astrology at this point in my life. I turned to the week my wife and friend left me in the dust. I can still feel the words written on that page. They went something like this: "if you are in a difficult relationship, not getting the treatment you deserve, let it end!" I was shocked; I almost dropped the book on the floor. How could this fifty-cent paperback writer be so accurate? This experience widened a doorway for me. I have been, and still am, an avid student, practitioner, and teacher of Astrology to this day. You may laugh, but this was a life-changing moment. I had to investigate this further. It was beyond coincidence. I have found Astrology to be an extremely wise investment. You can check out my monthly Astrology Video Predictions on my YouTube channel, 333magic9.

EMBARRASSMENT AND INFURIATION

Two other experiences correspond with this part of my story. The first is embarrassing, the second infuriating. I met a lovely woman who was a waitress at a nice restaurant in Jamestown. We started dating, which led to an intimate encounter. She was an attractive Leo woman, very generous with her affection, unlike my Scorpio ex-wife. One night after making love, I asked her, if I was any good at making love? It was part of my emotional devastation. Some women might have laughed at my question, but she didn't. She gently hugged me and whispered in my ear, "Oh, yes!" I can't believe I asked the question, and I am saddened, I had to. I had no self-confidence.

The other experience once again illuminated my understanding of the Catholic religion. I was living through a challenging time, and I needed help, healing, and counseling. I had few friends to talk to, as I had been living in Jamestown for a bit more than a year. I reached back into my heritage and went to the local Catholic Church. The priest was a nice man, and I asked for his help. I explained my wife had left me, and I needed guidance. His first question was, "Where were you married my son?" I replied, "In her church, the Episcopal Church in Old Westbury, Long Island." Without hesitation, he replied, "Well, don't worry my son, that marriage doesn't count in the eyes of the Church." Wow, did he miss the mark! My feelings about the Church were clarified. The Church and its rules were more important than the people. It's an attitude that persists today. It was the last time I went to a Catholic Church.

REBIRTH IN ROCHESTER

I was living the life of an emotionally dead man in Jamestown. I had to get out of there. I went to my regional manager in Rochester, New York, to tell him I was leaving the company, and moving back to New York City. I did not mention anything about my situation and a broken marriage. I did not know it, but he already was aware of the situation. It seems one of the other company managers in New Jersey, had seen my wife and former boss together. The word had gotten out! He was a kind man, and he offered me a job in the Rochester office. I accepted, but I had to find someone to fill my position in Jamestown before I could move. Luckily, I had made a friend in the business community. He was a financial advisor, and on the local business development council. He agreed to take the job. I would soon be on my way to my new job, and hopefully, a better situation. This opportunity awakened a sense of optimism for the future.

Rochester was full of potential. Eastman Kodak was the leading employer, and the city was quite vibrant. It had a great Arts community and lots of cultural events. There was one other exciting phenomenon. It seems a lot of people around my age, mid-20s to mid-30s, were going through divorces or coming out of relationships.

It set up an exciting social scene. There were plenty of single adults who were looking for love without wanting to be in a permanent relationship. I did meet a lot of interesting people and had several amazing experiences. They helped heal my emotional wounds a bit. However, the hurt I experienced blocked me from really opening up and trusting anyone. I was doing pretty well at work and had an active social life. I was starting to enjoy life. Ah! But fate had other plans for me.

It was my second year in Rochester. The main office in New Jersey sent an artist to our office. He was a talented man and would prepare artwork for clients to help grow the business. However, he was also one of the most insecure people I have ever met. He had a big problem with alcohol. He reminded me of my father and the difficulties I experienced growing up. His presence made it almost impossible for me to do my job. One of my responsibilities was to develop new clients. Since we were a visual medium, we would show them a sample piece of artwork showing their potential ad. It is pretty typical in all forms of advertising. In Radio, you could do a spec spot, so a client could hear what it would sound like on air. In the TV business, you would present a storyboard. In Outdoor, if they could see what their billboard would look like, they'd be more open to buying space. Unfortunately, this man was so insecure; he wanted me to sit and watch him as he drew the spec artwork. He needed constant reinforcement. If you happened to run into him after his two martini lunch, it was a painful and frustrating experience. I had enough pain through my father; I did not need to experience this again.

I had the opportunity to make a presentation to a client who had never used Outdoor Advertising before. It was the largest radio station in Rochester, a 50,000 watt Clear Channel AM/FM combo. The station manager had asked me to make the presentation to the owner. The owner had never done any outside promotion like this before. In one 20-minute meeting, I sold him a substantial advertising package to run over several months. It was the largest sale I had ever made, and it would have enormous consequences. As I walked out of the presentation, the station manager followed me down the hall to the exit. Before I could leave, he said, "I want to see you in my office." "Uh, Oh!" I thought I'd done something wrong. When I sat down, he leaned over his desk and said, "Did you ever consider selling Radio? I have a sales position open, and I think you'd do a good job." I was a bit shocked and surprised. I declined. I stayed with the company I was working for because I did feel loyalty to them, and I knew nothing about the Radio. However, the conditions were getting worse. A few months went by, and I decided to give the radio station manager a call. I asked if the job was still open and his reply was "Yes, when do you want to start, tomorrow?" Again he surprised me. I told him I wanted to give my current employer two weeks' notice, and he agreed that it was proper. I would soon head in a new direction selling radio advertising.

   I was also studying and developing my talents in Psychic-Mediumship and Astrology. A few months after my job change, I bought a fascinating book, *The Eighth House, Sex and Death and Dollars*[8] by Marc Robertson. I looked back at what was happening astrologically during this time of change and struggle. I was going through a cycle called a Saturn return. It happens with varying effects for everyone between the ages of 28 and 30. I was also experiencing Saturn's transit of Pluto. I do not remember it exactly, but the reading said it was a good time to leave a situation that was deteriorating, for new and better potentials could lead to a more powerful position. That was right on! I went from selling Outdoor Advertising to working at the most powerful radio station in the market. I took a step toward a greater future. It would lead me to work in and on television a few years later.

   Things were finally going well. I was almost immediately successful. I found my niche. In a few short months, I had taken a list of clients that were billing $7000 a month, to over $35,000 a month. I enjoyed the excitement, the challenge, and the rewards of being successful. I also found I had a talent for setting up promotions. At the same time, I continued studying Astrology. I had met a new friend, Ralph Lewis, a professional Psychic, Medium, and Astrologer. He introduced me to my spiritual teacher, the Reverend Harry Bender.

My social life also picked up. I met a nice young woman at one of our radio promotions. We got along so well; we were soon living together. I had made it very clear, because of my experience, I did not want to get married again. She had also come out of a complicated relationship, so she wasn't pushing for permanency either. Well, they say change is the only constant in life, and it soon came again.

The radio station owner brought in a new management team. Unfortunately, they were not very good managers. This happened to me several times in sales, the more successful you are, the more they take away from you. I will never understand this. If you are working at a 10% commission, they make 90% of the sale. It would seem the more you sell, the happier they should be. However, they don't want you to be too successful. It makes no sense. The atmosphere was tense, and I would soon be on my way to another job. While this was going on, there was a woman out of Chicago, Irene Hughes, who was doing call-in psychic readings on a competing radio station, WBBF. Since I was studying psychic and spiritual development with my teacher, and beginning to do psychic readings, I was fascinated by her talents. Little did I know within the year, I would replace her on air. My next sales job was at WBBF. If change is constant, there is a lot of constancy in the radio business.

I did very well in sales for the first year. I was also invited to be part of the morning drive show on Thursday mornings. People would call in, and I would give each caller a live on-air psychic reading. My appearances were very successful. During the second week, the telephone company called the station and asked if they were running a big giveaway. The phone lines were overloaded — not a bad compliment. But again, change came knocking. WBBF was a 1000 watt AM station, and FM stations were on the rise. Until now, FM was almost a secondary thought in the broadcasting business. But just like Cable TV and the Internet brought radical change to the media, the quality of the FM signal, especially with rock music, shook up the world of Radio. Since I was working on the AM side, I, like the other salespeople, took a big hit as advertising spending moved with the audiences to FM. At the same time, the woman I was living with had finished her degree and was offered a job in Albany, New York. Since my income had halved, and the pressure for more sales by a very poor manager doubled, I decided it was time to seek greener pastures. I quit my job and moved with my significant other to Albany. I would be there for about a month without a position. However, I had interviewed with a Radio and a TV station. I wanted to get into TV because I could see it was much more powerful than Radio. The funny thing is, I had job offers from both on the same day. I chose the TV account executive job because I wanted to learn the medium, but also because of the promises the sales manager made. Little did I know his promises were just out and out lies. Struggle again!

CRUSHED AGAIN BY LOVE

The woman I was living with was happy in her new job. She was a social worker and interpreter for the deaf. It was a more satisfying and rewarding position than selling advertising, but not very lucrative. We all have our challenges. One of hers would come through her mother. Her mom and dad were pleasant people. I got along well with them, and they liked me. Our first year in Albany past quickly. Then, bad news hit! Her father received a diagnosis of cancer. It was fast-moving, so this was a sad and devastating time. Understandably, her mother was taking it very hard. However, she made it even more difficult. She wanted both of her daughters to get married before their father died. I was not aware of this demand, but it put a lot of pressure on our relationship. Rather than being open about what her mom had said, and discussing it with me, she must have been afraid she would lose me. Instead, she tried to motivate me through jealousy. She invited one of her male associates into our apartment and entertained him under the guise of business. She repeated this several times and went out to meetings with him at night. She was also turning colder in her feelings and actions toward me. I guess I can be a little thick. After a few weeks of this, lacking the reaction she had hoped for, and still, under pressure from her mother, she dropped the "Marry me or else bomb!" That was not a wise choice, and it didn't end well.

I had to say, "Or else!" How could you live with someone who tried to manipulate you in that way? I was incredibly devastated when we broke up, but I didn't feel I had any choice but to stand my ground. Once trust is lost, it would be hard to repair the relationship. There would always be the "or else" as a possible tool in the future. The great sadness of this experience is, it hurt both of us. I knew she still loved me because she visited me several years later. You can tell when someone loves you. But her actions put another dagger in my heart. It reawakened such a depth of sorrow and depression; I could not even get excited by a woman for over four years. I was broken once again by love and the emotional ruthlessness of a woman. I know in today's world, women are joining the "Me Too" movement to combat the physical and manipulative abuse from men in power. I support that movement. Any type of manipulation or abuse of power is unworthy. However, my experience has come from the other direction. I think there should be a "Me Also" movement for men who have been brutalized and emotionally devastated by women they've loved. Men usually don't understand the emotional power of women. It goes way back to the Genesis story of Adam, Eve, and the Serpent. The Serpent is the emotional and sexual energies that can ruin any relationship. There goes Paradise!

Life goes on, and the constancy of change struck again. The TV station I was working at hired a new manager. He wanted to make his mark on the world. He called a meeting with the sales team in January to announce a new compensation plan. The commission rate changed from 8 percent to 3.5. He also added four new sales quotas per month. He was a stupid man. It takes a few years for a TV Account Executive to know the business, and become successful. It only took a few months, but two of us left the company. They had stolen over $10,000 from my commissions in 6 months; the other salesman lost more. The silver lining in the dark cloud was it forced me to start my own business. I had never wanted to have my own business, since I had grown up in a family business, and knew the pitfalls. However, as one door closed, many new opportunities would open in different areas of my life. What a year! Lost a woman I loved, and lost a successful and lucrative job. Two years later, I had a lunch meeting with the new Station Manager, who replaced the idiot. He had been the Business Manager at the TV station when I worked there. He told me in the two years since we left the station, they had lost over 2 million in sales. They gained a few thousand by cutting our commissions but lost 2 million. That manager was not a bright light.

Many new and different opportunities came my way after leaving the TV station. (One door closes, and another opens.) In the next few years, I grew my small Advertising Agency; published my first book, *The Art of the Mystic*[9]; did numerous radio shows; traveled to and served many Spiritualist Churches and Camps; helped organize the American Federation of Spiritualist Churches; completed our three-year course, and became an Ordained Minister. Some unexpected angels brought blessings into my life. It often happens when you are walking a spiritual path. During this time, I lectured at a number of our churches. Since I was interested in the different religions and how they express their beliefs, I decided to go back to school and take a course in comparative religions. That way, I would be more confident about what I was saying. I enrolled in an undergraduate course at the University at Albany.

The professor was fabulous. You could tell he loved teaching and opening the minds of young students. His name was Thomas Martland, and he used his book, *Religion as Art*[10] in the class. His approach is a comparison between the expressive nature of religion and art and how they offered a new approach to understanding the world. At the end of the semester, I gave him a copy of my book, *The Art of the Mystic* and decided to come back the next semester to take a course he was teaching on Existentialism. A few weeks into the second semester, he invited me out to lunch at the faculty club. I had no idea what he wanted to discuss. Over lunch, he said to me, "Tom, right now you're an Astrologer and a Psychic. When people hear you speak (He was talking from the viewpoint of academia), they say, listen to that jerk! I replied, I don't care what they think about me; I know what I know. He held up his hand to stop me and continued, "listen to me for a minute. What you need is a Ph.D." I immediately answered, "Where the heck am I going to get a Ph.D.! I'm 35 years old and have a business to run." He said, "Hear me out!" The conversation went like this. I am the chair of the graduate studies program here in the philosophy department. I have watched you interact with students who are 15 to 20 years younger than you are in the classroom. You listen to their opinions, and you treat them with respect. I think you would make a great professor. I again started to protest because of the responsibilities of running my own business. He held up his hand to stop me again and continued; I will recommend you for the Master's program here at the University at Albany. If you are successful here and can meet all the requirements, I have also sat an honored chair at Syracuse University School of Religious Studies. I will recommend you for their Ph.D. program. Then Tom, when you speak, they will say, "Listen to that jerk! But they will have to listen!" What an amazing opportunity. Unfortunately, I could not pursue the terminal degree, but I was able to complete my Master's Degree. Blessings and angels do come in surprising ways. This blessing would lead to another.

I did my Masters' thesis as a comparison between Plato's Theory of the Forms and the metaphysical theory of the Buddha. It was a challenge. The Buddha did not teach metaphysics. When faced with metaphysical questions that one cannot answer, he said, "Don't waste your time with questions you cannot answer. Follow the Eightfold Path to salvation." Approximately a year after completing my Masters, I walked into a copy center in Latham, New York to make some copies. Latham is a small suburb outside of Albany. I heard a commotion in the back room, and when I looked, I was surprised to see a Buddhist nun trying to use one of the copy machines. My initial thought was, "What the hell is a Buddhist nun doing in Latham, New York?"

I walked over, helped her make the copies she needed, and as a gesture of kindness paid for them. Buddhist nuns don't usually have a whole lot of money. Her name was Jun Yasuda, and she was from Japan. The next day I got a copy of what she was mailing out. It was an invitation to the *Grafton Peace Pagoda*[11]. At that time the Peace Pagoda was beginning construction. I went to see what it was about.

Volunteers were doing the work. What a great blessing! I was allowed to help build a beautiful Buddhist monument to peace. I mixed cement by hand, washed rocks, and did carpentry work. As I would learn, "Jun Sun" is an exceptional being.

I jokingly call her my Mother Theresa. The lessons I learned through volunteering my time and energy helped me open my heart, and give to projects that were more important than my personal needs and desires. Spending time with Jun Sun has had a profound effect on my understanding of spirituality in action. I hope you take the time to look up the Grafton Peace Pagoda on the Internet. I uploaded a beautiful video onto YouTube of Jun Sun chanting the Lotus Sutra "Lotus Sutra at the Grafton Peace Pagoda." It is truly a beautiful place that has impacted the lives of thousands of people. I hope you will have the opportunity to find a Peace Pagoda on your life path.

A debt of gratitude goes to both Thomas Martland and Jun Yasuda, gifts on the path of life.

ANOTHER PRIESTLY MOMENT

It's Catholic time again. I had become an ordained minister in the Religion of Spiritualism. Ordination allowed me to perform weddings. Several couples had come to me for private readings and compatibility work. Astrology can give great insight into relationship issues based on the energy interaction between two people. They liked my approach and guidance. They also wanted me to perform their wedding services. One stands out, for its beauty, location, and a rather odd occurrence. The wedding was to be at the bride's mother's house on the shores of Blue Mountain Lake, a beautiful lake in New York's Adirondack Park. There was a large dinner Saturday night at one of the old Adirondack hunting camps across the lake. It had been beautifully restored by Syracuse University. It is a truly exquisite location, and It had a commanding view of the lake. We had a fabulous dinner, and the lodge was inhabited by large mounted animals that captured the spirit of a hunting camp. The dinner went well, and all retired to various motels and cottages to rest up for the big wedding day. I had prepared the service with the couple a few weeks earlier. But, there was one unusual request. The bride's mother was Catholic. She wasn't happy a Spiritualist Minister was officiating the service, rather than a priest. The couple agreed to a special prayer by a priest to bless the wedding to make her feel more comfortable. It was fine with me. I understood because I also had a Catholic mom.

I was staying in the hamlet of Blue Mountain Lake. I got up early to take a morning walk. As I was walking in the village, I ran into a bear having breakfast at a restaurant's dumpster. I was a bit surprised but gave him plenty of space, and he did the same. I bid him good morning and was on my way. I think he represented something old as associated with the wedding, but in this experience, a religious attitude. I arrived at the lakefront house for the wedding a bit early. I was talking with some of the guests on the lawn. I was dressed in a suit and tie, as I don't like clerical attire. Can you imagine Jesus walking around in a bright and shiny robe? Robes tend to differentiate the minister from the people. Jesus mingled with the people. The Catholic priest approached me, and without even introducing himself, asked me the following question: "Are you a real minister?" Wow, what arrogance! If I had not experienced it, I would not have believed it. Boom, the old Catholic Bomb! Are they really that ignorant? They must think they are better than everyone else.

I was kind and just said yes. I did not address the question with a qualifying answer. He had no right to know. The couple knew who I was, and they had selected me to officiate at their wedding. This priest suffered from the arrogance of the Catholic Church, and the fear it imposes on its believers. The mother of the bride and the priest are good examples of that fear. They reawakened so many bad memories. However, the drama wasn't quite over. At the end of my wedding service, I offer a special blessing. It goes something like this: I invite everyone to be joined in prayer to bless the newlyweds. I start my prayer by saying, "Great Spirit, this is your son Thomas . . ." before I could finish the blessing prayer, the mother of the bride let out a loud gasp! Another Catholic Bomb! You could have heard a pin drop. Undaunted, I continued my blessing as usual. "I am here today with the family and friends of (the couple) we are all your children . . ." Don't they teach we are all children of God? This worried woman must have thought I was trying to take the role of Jesus. I never said or implied that but her fear and ignorance compelled her reaction, and she interrupted a lovely blessing.

POSTGRADUATE

Back to school. I was extremely fortunate to attend Graduate School at the University at Albany. It was a fabulous learning experience. I also met another woman, or I should say she met me. She came into one of the graduate classes I was attending and dropped her books on my feet. That was not a mistake. She was trying to meet me. It turned out she was a missy - a selfish and spoiled woman. She was smart and attractive, but also narcissistic. I wound up living with her and had hope for some happiness together. However, that didn't happen. I knew it wasn't great, but I had hope. Her selfishness, and pressure from her family to leave, or they would cut her off financially were probably too much, and she did go. It was inevitable. But the way she did it was heartless.

She had a part-time job with the State of New York. We shared a computer at home. I do a lot of writing on Astrology and for my other business responsibilities. Things were rocky between us as she was happy to take, but not overly warm or giving. However, her prearranged and abrupt departure surprised me. I had to travel to Boston to attend a conference and do a church service, so I was going to stay overnight. It's over three hours each way according to traffic and weather conditions. I invited her to come for the weekend. Boston can be a lot of fun. I was surprised when she declined, but she did have a lot of work to do, so I didn't overthink it. This was before the cell phone era. I left Boston and headed home on Sunday afternoon. I was three miles from our apartment. Suddenly, I had an overwhelming feeling. I almost drove off the road. I can't explain it any other way. I felt I'd been raped! I mean, physically raped! I had to stop the car to compose myself because I was so unnerved. I regained some composure and continued home. When I arrived, I found she had moved out of our apartment and taken all my work with her. It was a vicious act of manipulation and emotional terrorism. She could have easily copied my work to a disk and left it on the desk with a note. She didn't do that. What she wanted was to have power and control over the situation. Why not, it was happening to her. Oh well! Onward and upward.

A lesson learned. Relationships can be challenging. Look at the number of divorces, and people living alone. The numbers speak for themselves. If you are in a difficult relationship and need to leave it, try to do so with kindness and gentleness. Relationships are an area of high Karma. They are full of emotional baggage. Emotional baggage will travel with you for a long time and is difficult to heal. However, if you are in a bad relationship, where someone is harming you on a physical, emotional, psychological, or spiritual level, get out now! Don't look back! If you are the perpetrator of harm, stop now! The energy you are releasing is destructive to the person you are involved with but ultimately may destroy you. A relationship is an emotional bond based on the power of love. The opposite of love is hate. "Then said Jesus unto him, Put up again thy sword into his place: for all they that take the sword shall perish with the sword." (Matthew 26:52) It is the essence of the Law of Karma: As you sow! Its bonds intensify with emotional power.

I share these experiences with you from my heart. They are the wealth of my life.

Thomas F. Kearns

CHAPTER 4 - FREEING JESUS

A WALK WITH JESUS

Jesus should have hired a Scribe. He had so many interactions with them. If he had, we might have clear reporting about what he did, said, and taught. As it stands, in the study of the New Testament, there is much disagreement as to the words Jesus said, the words attributed to him, and what he did. Even Einstein wanted to know what was in the mind of God. If he wanted to know, it suggests he didn't. He was a smart man, and his interest illustrates how difficult it is to understand what God: was, is, and will be thinking. You might want to ask yourself: Would an all-loving God, send his son to be brutally tortured, mutilated, and killed? Was this an act of salvation? In a simple act of love, compassion, and kindness God could have forgiven everyone. Why the bloodthirsty high drama, when it was unnecessary? Think of the message of brutality gleaned from the life and passion of Jesus. Think of the effect it had on humanity, and still does to this day. If the actions of the religions of the book had followed the all-loving theme, the world would be very different.

Christianity has enormously influenced the world. But most people only understand Christianity through what they have learned from Christian ministry. If you take your beliefs seriously, you should be willing to look at the source of Christian teaching openly and honestly. Consider the different positions unearthed by recent scholarship. You may gain a different understanding through the work of the Jesus Seminar. They have published several critical studies on the veracity of the New Testament. Two are most interesting: *The Five Gospels - The Search for The Authentic Words of Jesus* and *The Acts of Jesus: What Did Jesus Really Do?*[12]

The Jesus Seminar led me to the writings of Bart Ehrman. I have struggled with my "Catholic" problem for a long time. When I found the work of Bart Ehrman and read about his story and spiritual struggle, I found someone with whom I could identify. His work became a light in the darkness for me, and it helped alleviate much of the suffering I had experienced through religion. In a sense, my spiritual wrestling with God healed. I was set free. I highly recommend his work to anyone who is questioning their faith versus the reality of religious teaching and practice. The ones I enjoyed the most were, *Misquoting Jesus: The Story Behind Who Changed the Bible and Why* and *Jesus, Interrupted: Revealing the Hidden Contradictions in the Bible (and Why We Don't Know About Them)*.[13] I am pro Jesus and anti-Christian. It may sound contradictory, but the many disagreements concerning the content and writing of the New Testament by scholars, historians, and theologians, make it clear. What we have learned for 2000 years about Jesus and the formation of Christianity, may not be valid. In this regard, *The Mythmaker, Paul and the Invention of Christianity*[14] by Hyam Maccoby, will give you a very different version of the formation of Christianity.

There are many things I would like to ask Jesus about his ministry. I imagine almost every Christian would love the opportunity to walk and talk with Jesus. Some, who would not, would probably be afraid of him, and to borrow Søren Kirkegaard's title, would act with *Fear and Trembling*[15] in his presence (what a shame!). Kahlil Gibran's *The Prophet*[16] may speak to this better when he describes the trembling of the shepherd who is to be honored by the king. Even a non-believer might find the opportunity amazing. Why a walk? Jesus spent most of his time walking around the towns and countryside. He did not need a 54 million-dollar jet, and neither did his disciples. They were explicitly instructed to take little with them when they went out to teach all nations. Imagine the Christian ministers of today doing that? Jesus walked, mingled, and talked to people. He usually taught informally, using stories, parables, questions, and answers. Jesus taught by example as well. Sometimes he taught large groups. There were multitudes, but that is a questionable description. Sometimes, he only taught his disciples, often concerning secret teachings. (Matthew 13:10-11, Mark 4:10-11, Luke 8:9-10) They didn't seem to learn much if we look at their actions and his comments about them. The descent of the Holy Spirit was needed to help them understand. Yet, the simplicity of walking through the countryside, listening to words of wisdom and deliverance from a Master is quite compelling.

Walking with Jesus would also allow us to see beyond the mere words we now read. Words do have tremendous power, but we would have the opportunity to feel the experience, identify with Jesus, and savor the moments. We could see Jesus holding the coin when he answers the Scribes and Pharisees, "Render to Caesar the things that are Caesar's, and to God the things that are God's" (Mark 12:17, Matthew 22:21). We could see the disgraced woman when the men brought "The Woman Caught in Adultery" before Jesus. (John 8:3-11) We could feel his compassion and wisdom as he told her, "Go and sin no more." (John 8:11) This story is compelling and has serious implications. The Old Testament teaches "And the man that committeth adultery with another man's wife, even he that committeth adultery with his neighbour's wife, the adulterer and the adulteress shall surely be put to death." (Leviticus 20:10)

There are many reasons "The Woman Caught in Adultery" is a favorite New Testament story. It occurs as Jesus is going to the Mount of Olives to teach. It demonstrates the wisdom of Jesus, the evil nature of the woman's accusers "He who is without sin among you, let him first cast a stone at her." (John 8:7) (an admonition ignored by most), and the power of compassion and forgiveness. Wouldn't we all want to be told, "go, and sin no more." by Jesus? (John 8:11) Combined, a double warning against judging, which is so prevalent in the Christian community. (Matthew 7:1-3) Christian leadership, ministers, and teachers must never have read these passages, as they seem happy and eager to judge. Perhaps, they might know something about their veracity; I do not know. Another reason is it shows how smart Jesus was. My teacher, the Reverend Harry Bender of Rochester, New York, often said, "Jesus was a brilliant man." Wouldn't we all like to catch our enemies with such clear logic? Another reason is, it takes me back to the Book of Genesis, where again a woman is a scapegoat. More about that story later.

Like many Old and New Testament stories, "The Woman Caught in Adultery" is perplexing. We know little about the woman, the man who participated in the adultery is not present, so we don't know anything about him, and we also know little about the accusers. All we know is they are Scribes and Pharisees, and we know they are trying to trick Jesus. Jesus is known for his teaching of "Good News" and forgiveness, yet adultery is against the Law of Moses. It demands the guilty participants be stoned to death when they are caught in the act. Furthermore, and interestingly, Jesus strictly enforces the sacredness of marriage vows, contradicting the accepted cultural practice of divorce when he says, "What therefore God hath joined together, let not man put asunder." (Mark 10:9)

Before looking at some of the possible meanings and interpretations of this story, let us go back in time to the Old Testament. Stories in the Old and New Testaments are often linked with one another. The first time I heard the following lecture was at the Plymouth Spiritualist Church in Rochester, New York. My teacher, the Reverend Harry Bender, delivered it at a Sunday service in the early 1970s. He was the Pastor of the Church. He had a very unusual way of interpreting scripture. He helped open my eyes and mind to different possibilities, and perhaps his teaching on Genesis will help you in your process of understanding, especially if you question "The Truth" and you are a seeker.

LECTURE ON GENESIS

Theologians, anthropologists, and geologists disagree as to the age of man, but all agree he is much older than Adam and Eve. In the study of anthropology, we are of the genus called Homo sapiens and about 150,000 years old. The Old Testament suggests that Cain went forth and dwelt in the Land of Nod about 6,000 years ago. In their great debate in 1925, William Jennings Bryan and Clarence Darrow were not able to bring together the thinking of science and theology. We are still-witness to the discussion today with science versus Creationism. If these two learned men could not agree, nor those learned men of today, then let us set aside our accumulated wisdom of the ages, and read the Bible in as simple a manner as possible, using neither a theological nor a scientific outlook.

In the first chapter of Genesis, we find, "In the beginning, God created the heaven and the Earth." (Genesis 1:1) We can assume this means the Universe. God, Jehovah, Yahweh, Allah, The Great Spirit, Infinite Intelligence - call it what you will, but in the beginning, God created the heavens and the earth. Theology teaches us there was a beginning. Science also shows us; our Universe was created at one time. It was either an enormous explosion, the big bang or implosion, that led to the formation of the Universe.

"And God said, Let there be light: and there was light." (Genesis 1:3) I don't think it would take much of a science teacher to tell you the Sun, Moon, and Stars are in the heavens. God said, "Let the waters under the heaven be gathered together unto one place, and let the dry land appear: and it was so." (Genesis 1:9) Science teaches us that in the beginning, the world was without form, a gaseous blob, the gases turned to vapor, and the vapor to water. Due to volcanic action and crust movement, the waters divided and the land appeared.

After the first nineteen verses in the first chapter of Genesis, we could say we come to a parting of the ways of thinking. At this time, I say to you, let's keep our minds clear and free from all things, both scientific and religious. Verse 20 tells us: "And God said, Let the waters bring forth abundantly the moving creature that hath life," Is not this a condensation of the theory of evolution? In other words, the theory of evolution says that in the beginning, all life comes through the waters.

The Law of Genetics is so essential it is mentioned no less than six times in the first chapter of Genesis. The Law of Genetics states each should bring forth its own kind. A disturbance of the Law of Genetics would bring forth a hybrid creature. A good example is the breeding of a horse and a jackass. If you breed a horse with a jackass (two different species), the result is a mule. The mule is a hybrid creature. All mules are female, and all mules are sterile. They can't reproduce. If you disturb the Law of Genetics, the Law of Nature steps in and cancels it. Therefore, each creature must progress or evolve with its kind. It seems safe to say, according to scientific findings and the postulates of theology, man evolved from man-creature and animals from animals. Over thousands of years, it stands to reason there must be one kind of creature that is outstanding above all others. We call this creature, man. Verse 27 tells us God created man, male and female, both sexes at the same time. "So God created man in his own image, in the image of God created he him; male and female created he them." Man must have been a part of creation or evolution. Science says this is true according to genetics.

Verses 28 and 29 tell us this creature man was given specific tasks to do, such as multiply, replenish, and subdue the earth. He was given specific things to eat. We find these traits in civilization today. Don't forget your genes. You know that you are male or female. We've all seen many people who seem to have no other thought except to eat, drink, and populate the earth. If you haven't seen this, you've been leading a very secluded life. Up to this point, nothing is said concerning the spirit. You can read the first chapter of Genesis over and over, and you won't find one word that says anything about spiritual matters. Therefore, you must be a product of nature, or a product of evolution.

Since man's only actual needs were supplied by nature, his gods would necessarily be of nature. He was not given the breath of God or spiritual soul. It helps explain prehistoric paintings found in caverns and places which contain the forms of worship of ancient man. They were always of nature. This created man multiplied, formed into units or tribes, and migrated to every part of the earth to fulfill its mission: to eat, drink, and populate the earth. The Divine plan of evolution is fixed in its course. Verse 31 plainly states everything is "very good."

Remember, in creation; everything is very good. This ends the sixth day of creation, and we also include the seventh day on which God rested. We have covered many, many thousands of years.

Now, you have to speculate. If God (God is spirit) selected man to be the physical manifestation of Himself, a way had to be found, or made, for the spirit of God to enter into this man of evolution, and still be in accord with the Law of Genetics. After the earth had been created or made, it is written, there was not a man to till the ground. This statement points out that the created man was a man of nature or a man of evolution. Let us consider the phrase "to till the ground" in the vernacular of today. The salesman going into virgin territory is said to be opening "new fields." "Keep a steady hand on the plow" or "plow a straight furrow" were common expressions in the past. So, to till the ground doesn't mean a farmer is needed, but more likely, men were beginning to express their spiritual ideas, rather than those of nature.

The people who use the Bible as a base of their religion believe, as people in other spiritual beliefs, man has within himself a spiritual being. It is the soul, or it may be called spirit. You can put your label on it, but there is something within yourself that is missing from other creatures. Whatever you call it, according to the Genetic Law of each bringing forth its own kind, the man of nature does not possess the quality. The only quality the man of nature had, that is not present in the other created creatures who came from the waters is intelligence. The other created animals did not have intelligence. They only had instinct. With the ability to think, this created man was able to subdue the earth and prepare himself to receive the spiritual quality, fulfilling the teachings of the spiritual religions of today. A way must be provided so that this spiritual quality could be changed by natural law, into a material quality, and yet hold spirituality. This being must be able to breed with the created man and still be entirely in accord with the Law of Evolution.

My use of the word "law" may be confusing to you. A law cannot change or be changed. We say we govern our country by law. It is not governed by law, but by rules. You can change a rule, but you cannot change a law. The Law of Gravity, regardless of where you find it in the Universe, always operates the same way. It cannot change. You cannot violate it. You can overcome it, but only by using another law. As an example, the Law of Aerodynamics can be used to overcome the effects of the Law of Gravity.

Now we go to the second chapter of Genesis, and we find something entirely different. In verse 2:7, we find "And the Lord God formed man of the dust of the ground, and breathed into his nostrils the breath of life; and man became a living soul." Here is a different kind of man. This man is formed, not created. Created man is found in the first chapter, and in the second chapter, man is formed. This man is formed by God. He does not come from the water, yet he is manlike. Using the knowledge we have today, we can reason it is possible to use positive and negative electrons to form matter.

God formed man from the dust of the earth. The dust of the earth is not dirt; it is the atom. Individual atomic particles can build a form, that would not have substance but yet have energy. Here is the kicker. "and breathed into his nostrils the breath of life, and man became a living soul." (Genesis 2:7) What does this say? It doesn't say anything about man becoming flesh. It says man became a living soul. A soul does not have substance as we understand it. Call it spirit if you like. Therefore, this formed man must have been an ethereal being. A spiritual part is prepared eastward in Eden. Or, if you turn to Genesis 2:8, you'll find this Eden or paradise. In Eden stands the Tree of Life and the Tree of Knowledge. It was here that God put the man he wanted, not the created man. The created man could not go there anyway. Created man is a physical being, and this is a spiritual place.

"It is not good that the man should be alone;" (Genesis 2:18). God made a woman out of one of Adam's ribs. Think carefully about this. This line gives us a wealth of information. This formed man has a name, whereas the created man did not have a name. "It is not good for the man to be alone," and although this formation is following spiritual laws, the Law of Genetics must be kept in mind. The seed of both male and female of the same species are needed to produce their own kind.

There are people today, who believe the solar plexus area of the human body is an important psychic center from which a substance called ectoplasm can be created. It can be utilized to build a translucent form that has energy, but not substance. It is said you have to be in deep sleep or trance to produce this phenomenon. I may have used words that some of you may not understand, but you will, before the end of my course. God, therefore, created a woman by using ectoplasm (or energy) from the solar plexus of Adam. For the created man of nature to become God-like, he must have a part of God instilled into his being, or the breath of God, or both. This must follow Natural Law, each to bring forth his own kind. Remember, this law is so important it is mentioned at least six times in the first chapter of Genesis.

At this point, we have the created man and woman, and Adam and his counterpart who will be named Eve. They were ethereal beings. It was not feasible to breed a physical man with a spirit. The Virgin Mary did it, but only through divine intervention. The only possible solution was to provide a way the living souls could be given a flesh body, yet retain the breath of life. Then, and only then, could this part of God be passed on to the created man, and still stay within the Law of Evolution.

I have always given women credit for being smarter than men. The woman must have known that there was a purpose, or plan, that had something to do with the Tree of Knowledge. And so it came to pass she went to a talking serpent. It does not say snake or viper, but a talking serpent. She went to a talking serpent that had great wisdom for counseling. In some of the other religions, people learn about such a Serpent. He has been called "Kundalini" "Serpent of Wisdom" or "Serpent of Fire." The Serpent, being very wise, must also have known of the plan, and advised them to eat of the fruit saying "Ye shall not surely die:" (Genesis 3:4) Notice I did not mention an apple, because it doesn't say anything about an apple. She also gave the fruit to her husband, and they died. Death here represents a change of condition.

If you have a Christian background, you are taught that when you die, you transcend from a material to a spiritual body. That is the way you become a spirit - you lay down and stop breathing. Therefore, Adam and Eve, or Adam and the woman (being spiritual), must have transcended from the spiritual to the material. At any rate, we know something occurred, because they became aware they were naked. How did they know they were naked? (Genesis 3:7) A possible solution is they had eaten some material substance, or they did something that transformed them into a physical body. What had been a mass of energy had gathered together into a material being or a body. It now had knowledge.

Adam and his counterpart woman were now flesh. They had the same type of body as the created man, but there was a difference. They had within themselves the indwelling spirit, soul, or breath of life. At this time, the woman became a personality. She was known as Eve, the "Mother of all living." (Souls) (Genesis 3:20) And God made them coats and clothed them to protect their flesh bodies from the elements of nature. This could not have been an angry God, but a God that was so pleased, He came to His children bearing gifts. "Therefore the Lord God sent him forth from the Garden of Eden, to till the ground from whence he was taken." (Genesis 3:23) As to verse 24, did you ever drive your family into the country for the day, drive a friend home, drive yourself to do a better job, or drive over to someone's house who needed help?

Eve began her mission on Earth by giving birth to Cain and Abel. She was to be the Mother of all living (souls). These children had within their being the blessing of the indwelling spirit or soul. Cain killed Abel. This act may be the first sin. "Thou shalt not kill" (Exodus 20:13) The only people at this time are Adam, Eve, Cain, and the created men and women (They were to populate the Earth). Cain must now start the process that will fulfill Eve's mission. He is to find a mate in the Land of Nod. Following the law, Cain is a man with a soul, and man can breed with a woman, bringing forth a man. It stands to reason that since each brings forth its own kind, then every descendant of Adam and Eve, through Cain or any of their other children, must have within them a part of God we call soul. All ministers, of all spiritual religions, teach that within man there is something no other creature of the Earth has. If you believe this something, a part of God, is within you, then you must believe you are God-like. Take advantage of this thought, and live in accord with your heritage.

COMMENTARY ON GENESIS

I will add a few comments about Harry's lecture. The first time I heard him deliver it, I was entranced. I grew up as a devout and conservative Catholic. My high school yearbook picture was me taking Holy Communion. I was going to be the priest of the family. It doesn't mean I was holy or anything like that, but I was indoctrinated. I had heard many a lecture on selected passages from the scriptures. We listened to the stories and studied the catechism, but not the scriptures themselves. They taught us selectively. I had never experienced anything like Harry's interpretation of Genesis. It perplexed me at first but also opened my mind to different possibilities. I look at this story now and see other alternate meanings. The first and perhaps most important is the concept of original sin.

Religion teachers tell us Adam and Eve disobeyed God. But could the sin of Adam and Eve be disobedience, or something else? Does a little child have the understanding necessary to sin? Adam and Eve were innocent. They had no experience, training, or education. They were "tabula rasa" before eating of the fruit of the knowledge of good and evil, right or wrong. They weren't capable of sinning. They had no awareness of good, evil, obedience, and disobedience. Why would an all-knowing, and especially all-loving God, hold them to this measure? If we look closely at the story, we see a more remarkable possibility. The supposed sin is one of gaining awareness, not disobedience. The fruit of the tree was the knowledge of good vs. evil, or in other terms, the realization of the dualism of God's creation. Jesus taught, "Judge not, that ye be not judged." (Matthew 7:1) Perhaps he taught this because he realized, all creation came from God. How could anything God created be wrong, and how could we ever understand it, if it was? God, is a mystery, and beyond our capability to understand. Adam and Eve did not create dualism in the world. But like all of us, they were surely under its influence. Oriental or Eastern Philosophy describe it as Yin and Yang. It is a complementary, interactive, and balanced condition.

There is another remarkable event at the end of this story. It seems God is afraid humankind will become just like God. "Behold, the man is become as one of us, to know good and evil: and now, lest he put forth his hand, and take also of the tree of life, and eat, and live forever:" (Genesis 3:22) We must speculate about why God is afraid we will become "like one of us" if we are to understand this passage. Is God afraid man who has gained the knowledge of good and evil, will now gain the awareness he lives eternally "like one of us" Or, will we become all-powerful like God? Now that is a scary thought! Imagine 6 billion people running around the world, all of them as powerful as the Almighty Creator, but with very little self-control. The Old Testament tells us, "God is a jealous God." (Exodus 20:5) Perhaps this proves it. God, or more correctly "Gods" (Like one of us) are protecting their power. And isn't it interesting God uses the word "us." Here in the hallowed halls of the foundation of monotheism, Judaism, there is more than one God. This is blasphemy. And it far predates any idea of the trinity, a concept not even directly taught in the New Testament.

Eve is blamed for the fall in the Garden. The adultery is blamed on the woman in "The Woman Taken in Adultery." Does this imply women are weak or evil? Or, does this show prejudice against women? This same implication becomes even more disturbing as the bias against Mary Magdalene. She was referred to as a prostitute for centuries. It shows a long-lasting historical bias against women, is found in both Old and New Testaments. Some would say it is still alive and well in the Catholic Church and Christianity today. Why were the writers so afraid of the women of their day? Perhaps, this can be better understood if we take another peek back into Genesis. We may find an answer. "And I will put enmity between thee and the woman, and between thy seed and her seed; it shall bruise thy head, and thou shalt bruise his heel." (Genesis 3:15) I am not quite sure about the use of the words heel and head mentioned in this passage. I think this passage has more to do with sexuality and all the suffering it causes both in the head and the soul. The head may represent the emotions and the heel, the soul. It is also interesting to consider the role of women in bringing forth life. We'll have to ask Achilles about the heel, although the foot does represent wisdom as suggested in the sign Pisces (the sign of spirituality - soul). It connects the physical and spiritual worlds. The battle of the sexes - and sexual dysfunction had begun, or it got noticed.

THE WOMAN TAKEN IN ADULTERY

Let us return to the New Testament and take a tour of the story "The Woman Taken in Adultery." (John 8:3-11) Let's go beyond the words to see what other meanings exist. We may go outside the boundaries of the story. I want to make a few points. First, as I mentioned, if the woman is caught in adultery, it means a man committed adultery as well. It does take two to tango. Where is the man, and why is he not brought before Jesus? He is missing from the picture. It is a great injustice to the woman, and Jesus allows it to slide. He never even mentions the male participant in the sin, or questions where he is. Perhaps, this is a throwback to the attitude of evil perpetrated against Eve in the Garden. It also smells of the same odor as the false judgment against Mary Magdalene. (There are also incidences where Jesus does not respect, and even rejects his Mother, the Blessed Virgin Mary, the Queen of Heaven.) Jesus knows the accusers are trying to trick him. They are not interested in the woman, or the sin, or the man who also participated in the transgression. We must ask, is it more important for Jesus to deal with the accusers, or with justice itself? He bends down and writes in the sand and says to them, "He that is without sin among you, let him first cast a stone at her." (John 8:7) They melt away quietly. But we are never told what he wrote, and why they melt away, other than they were "convicted by their own conscience." (John 8:9)

Light from Water

They left the accused woman with Jesus. We must speculate, he either wrote their sins or words that showed them the truth about their souls, something that shamed them. Jesus uses shame against the Scribes and Pharisees many times in other passages. Jesus asks her, "Woman, where are those thine accusers? hath no man condemned thee?" (John 8:10) She answers, "No man Lord." Jesus says to her, "Neither do I condemn thee: go, and sin no more." (John 8:11) This story offers a very nice outcome for the woman and a win for Jesus over the Scribes and Pharisees. Unfortunately, there is evidence it never occurred or was added to the New Testament many years later.

Bible scholars point out this story was not in the original New Testament. There is no mention of it in the earliest copies of the New Testament available. It may have come from other sources, but it does not appear in copies until many years later. It is also important to remember; there are no original copies of the New Testament. Furthermore, there is debate among scholars as to who Mark, Matthew, Luke, and John were. Their names may be imaginary, Perhaps that is why the stories are imaginative as well.

If you are serious about your belief in Jesus or sincerely do not believe in Jesus, he is still a pivotal person in history. The vehicle of Christianity has been used to shape much of the world's culture. The Protestant Reformation, the importance of Christianity, and new research methods into its teachings have done much to illuminate what may be accurate and what may not be accurate in the New Testament. Since Christianity teaches the survival of your soul is dependent on whether or not Christianity and Jesus will stand up to the test of scientific scrutiny, wouldn't it be wise to investigate the truth of this critical study. Unfortunately, it is complicated, and if you don't want to dedicate your life to it, I think you can rely on the expert source material available for study both "pro" and "con." If you do want to go to the New Testament itself, follow the advice of Bart Ehrman. He tells you a logical way to test New Testament writings in his book "*Jesus Interrupted - page 70.*" It is a simple process to follow.

Scholars like Bart Ehrman, John Dominic Crossan, and members of the Jesus Seminar (as well as many before them) have done a great deal of meaningful work. I have already mentioned my favorite books by Ehrman. I also recommend: *The Birth of Christianity, Discovering what happened in the Years Immediately After the Execution of Jesus*[17] by John Dominic Crossan and the work of the Jesus Seminar. You may also find a Google search on Papyrus P52 enlightening. If you don't like to read, there are plenty of excellent and enlightening videos on YouTube, which cover these issues and more. It is a significant opportunity to listen to both sides of the debate, and they are enlightening.

Another fascinating visual aspect of "The Woman Taken in Adultery" passage is Jesus' writing on the ground. I am not an expert in the New Testament. Many experts have offered differing interpretations of his action. They range from the idea; he wrote their sins, biblical passages, or even the impression that he was doodling. One must recognize if what he wrote was important, important enough to shame the accusers away; the author of this story should have shared that information. Some scholars suggest this act represented a claim that Jesus could write. Only a small percentage of people knew how to read and write. How did he, coming from a small town, brought up in a country family, learn to read and write? I will not mention every story or parable in the New Testament - work done too many times and in too many versions. Ever wonder why, if the Bible is the "Word of God," there could be more than one version? Ponder that for a while. However, I would like to make some critical points on selected passages of the New Testament. I hope they are worthy of your consideration.

JESUS ON LOVE

"For God so loved the world, that he gave his only begotten Son, that whosoever believeth in him should not perish, but have everlasting life." (John 3:16) The New Testament tells us, God sent his Son, not to condemn, but to save the world. Jesus, through his words and actions, often demonstrated love. He teaches us about the importance and practice of love when he answers the Pharisee, an expert in the law. When asked, "what is the greatest commandment?" Jesus answers,

> Thou shalt love the Lord thy God with all thy heart, and with all thy soul, and with all thy mind. This is the first and great commandment. And the second is like unto it, Thou shalt love thy neighbour as thyself. On these two commandments hang all the law and the prophets. (Matthew 22: 37-40)

Jesus teaches everything that exists, thrives on the Law of Love. Jesus also went beyond this teaching in his many parables and examples. He also took the radical approach of teaching us to love our enemies (Matt 5:44), to turn the other cheek, and to help those in need without expecting anything in return. He tells us if we do these things, we will be children of the "Highest." (Luke 6:35) He even commands us, "That ye love one another; as I have loved you, that ye also love one another." (John 13:34-35) Can you imagine how wonderful this world would be if Christians followed these teachings for the past 2000 years? How many wars waged, and how many souls were killed in the name of Jesus? Christians even killed Christians in his names. How did that make Jesus feel as he suffered on the cross? Who will be judged more harshly, the molested child, or the priest who molested the child? These things happened in the name of Jesus. If you were a father and loved your son, would you make him a human sacrifice? Think about that concept. As the all-loving God, you could forgive anyone, or everyone, for everything, in less than a blink of an eye. Why was the brutality and torture of Jesus necessary?

In the parable of the Good Samaritan (Luke 10:30-37), Jesus gives an example of the shallowness of people who appear to be good. Both a priest and a Levite cross to the other side of the road when confronted with a victim. They do not want to assist the man who has been robbed and beaten. I have dealt with people like this. They wouldn't do business with me, because I was a Spiritualist. They were God-fearing Christians. Only the Good Samaritan goes out of his way to show mercy to the man. Jesus praises him! Would he honor the baker, who would not bake a cake for a gay couple? In the parable of the Lost Sheep, Jesus teaches God will persist, and go out of his way, to seek even one of the flock who has gone astray. However, in the New Testament, the Scribes and Pharisees, who have obviously "gone astray" are judged, vilified, and condemned. They are called vipers and snakes! Is this the language of love and forgiveness? The Good Shepherd parable is often depicted using a visual of Jesus carrying a lamb on his shoulders, returning it to the flock. Wouldn't it have been wonderful if Jesus carried (saved) one of the scribes? The Good Shepherd image probably finds its origin from an earlier Greek Myth expressed in the Epithet of Hermes, Hermes Kriophoros from the 4-century B.C. In the parable of the Prodigal Son, Jesus again teaches love, mercy, acceptance, and forgiveness. (Luke 15:11-32) Why didn't God show mercy on Jesus? Jesus asked for it when he was praying in the Garden.

Jesus is often called the Prince of Peace. He is the most important messenger of love and forgiveness. If his mission is to save sinners and return them to the fold, how could Jesus continually express discrimination and hatred towards anyone? Did He? Just consider the powerful contradiction in this passage:

> Whosoever therefore shall confess me before men, him will I confess also before my Father which is in heaven. But whosoever shall deny me before men, him will I also deny before my Father which is in heaven. Think not that I am come to send peace on Earth: I came not to send peace, but a sword. For I am come to set a man at variance against his father, and the daughter against her mother, and the daughter in law against her mother in law. (Matthew 10:32-35)

Key passages in the New Testament, do not appear to come from the God of Love or the Prince of Peace. Perhaps there is a different origin and purpose for this particular passage. Scholars have pointed out an environment of competition and distrust existed between the early Jewish followers of Jesus, and other more traditional

Jewish groups like the Scribes and Pharisees. There is a beautiful song in the musical *Fiddler on the Roof*[18] which may bring a bit of enlightenment to this passage. The song "Tradition" explains the customs of the Jews in Russia. The Scribes and Pharisees were promoting and protecting Jewish Tradition and family values in Judea at a time of real crisis. Their approach was a failure! The Jewish followers of Jesus were developing new and disturbing ideas with roots in a mystical past. Could there be a better way to differentiate Jesus and his teachings from the accepted norm? By destroying the importance of the fundamental traditional foundations of Jewish culture, Jesus was devaluing the teachings of the Scribes and Pharisees. God did not free the Jews from Roman oppression. A new approach was needed for salvation from this tyranny. God had promised a free Jewish state! Jesus "the Messiah" became the promise. A door opened, and a different concept appeared. However, bureaucracies almost always resist needed change. Let us take a look at the importance of marriage and divorce, and then hate!

JESUS ON DIVORCE

"What therefore God hath joined together, let not man put asunder." (Matthew 19:6) "And I say unto you, Whosoever shall put away his wife, except it be for fornication, and shall marry another, committeth adultery: and whoso marrieth her which is put away doth commit adultery." (Matthew 19:9) Jesus is steadfast when he teaches on divorce. He allows little wiggle room and little forgiveness. The Law of Moses permitted divorce, but Jesus disagreed. One has to wonder why? Especially considering some of his other statements where he mentions family members. "But he answered and said unto him that told him, Who is my mother? and who are my brethren?" (Matthew 12:48) and "If any man come to me, and hate not his father, and mother, and wife, and children, and brethren, and sisters, yea, and his own life also, he cannot be my disciple." (Luke 14:26) How can divorce be such an important issue, if people who follow Jesus, who tells us to love everyone, now tells us to hate those closest to us? You must hate your wife or husband to follow Jesus. Hasn't this teaching added to religious confusion and intolerance? A plague on the world!

Here is one of the mysteries of the New Testament: The absence of Joseph, the husband of Mary, and the guardian (not the father) of Jesus. The last we hear about him is when Jesus is in the Temple at age twelve. What happened to Joseph? Does anyone care? We know Jesus had siblings, both brothers, and sisters. It proves Joseph and Mary spent time together and made a family after Jesus was born, and Jesus grew up in that family. There are a few possibilities. Did Joseph die? That would explain his absence. Or, perhaps Joseph divorced Mary. Either way, Jesus would have grown up in a broken home. That would have affected his feelings on marriage and divorce, and anything that would disrupt the family, except following God.

JESUS ON HATE - THE BEATITUDES AND WOES

Over the years, I have had many bad experiences with Christians. Many seem to hate or fear people who do not share their views. I often wondered where the hate came from until I studied the New Testament more closely. The Beatitudes (Matthew 5:3-10) contain some of the most beautiful and compelling teachings of Jesus. They may have come from the voice of Jesus. They are part of the Sermon on the Mount. They may be seen as promises or perhaps cures for conditions, although there is no necessary treatment. The Meek do not have to do anything; they will receive the Earth. Each begins with the word "blessed." The Greek word for blessed can also be translated as happy or blissful. The implication is meek people, or poor in spirit people, etc. should not be concerned with the condition of their life, and neither should they try to do anything about it. They will automatically have a better situation promised by Jesus. Even though he also says, "For ye have the poor with you always." (Mark 14:7, Matthew 26:11 John 12:8) How can the poor be with us always, if there is to be a second coming and glory? Jesus also tells us to, "Behold the fowls of the air: for they sow not, neither do they reap, nor gather into barns; yet your heavenly Father feedeth them. Are ye not much better than they?" (Matthew 6:26) These statements are quite different from the Buddhist medical metaphor. It describes an underlying condition of life, suffering, and then gives an active prescription for the cure of the illness, through personal responsibility, practice, and following the Eight Fold Path.

There are also subtle but unmistakable prejudices contained in the Beatitudes, as in almost every religion or belief system. They are structural concepts in the long practice of Christianity having influenced Western culture for ages. It would also be complicated, or too lengthy, to categorize all the different ills of the human condition, so some are missing. The eight statements are both simple and powerful, but they carry an influence colored by discrimination and bias. Perhaps this is where the Christians find their attitudes. You may be a bit confused by this statement. You may ask yourself, how could the words of Jesus express discrimination and bias? How could he stir up hatred in people? Jesus is God! God is Love! I believe it will be clear when four of the Beatitudes are repeated in the Sermon on the Plain in Luke. The four woes contrast them. (Luke 6:24-26)

The four woes in Luke are attacks against the rich, the well-fed, those who are enjoying life, and those who are popular. Why this significant bias against people who are happy and prosperous? It is a perplexing question to answer, and it still affects society today. Just look at our current social and political climate. Politicians attack the rich all the time. However, isn't it interesting, these same politicians, who demonize the rich, are willing to take their money. Then the politicians tell us we should tax the rich because they are evil. Then the politicians give them tax loopholes. You will find this attitude reinforced in other passages in the New Testament. Jesus says, "It is easier for a camel to go through the eye of a needle, than for a rich man to enter into the kingdom of God." (Mark 10:25, Matthew 19:24) It is also implied in the passage, "the birds of the air . . ." (Matthew 6:26) If I were walking with Jesus, I might ask why he didn't add statements like "Blessed or happy are the rich who give freely to those in need, they understand and are witnesses to God's generosity." Or, "Happy are the strong who protect and uplift the weak; they are messengers of God's strength."

Can you imagine the impact these powerful messages could have had on people throughout the ages? They may have influenced people to be more generous and helpful. And perhaps, the churches wouldn't have to ask people for money all the time. Why did Jesus have such disdain against people who may have worked very hard to achieve success, and who might also be very generous with their resources? Look at the comments by Jesus on the widow who gives two pennies suggesting she has given so much more than others. (Mark 12:43, Luke 21:1-4) Perhaps she has. He tells the good man to sell all he has and give it to the poor. He even tells his disciples to take nothing with them when they go to teach. (Mark 6:8, Luke 9:3) What if there were no rich people? Is that what Jesus was after? Would there be any cathedrals, schools, or hospitals? Perhaps the real essence of his teaching was and is, no one should need money. However, who would donate money to worthy causes? Who would give the Christian minister 54 million-dollars for his new airplane? There are demons in commercial planes. Who would ever want to fly commercial? It brings us to a more critical issue.

MONEY AND CHRISTIANITY

A significant difference in the teachings of Jesus and the application of Christianity comes in the area of money. Jesus had disdain for money, if not outright hostility to people who had it. The churches founded in the name of Jesus, or at least Christianity in general, seem to have no such qualms. Christians are thrilled and eager to ask for people's money. They are even willing to use buckets to collect it in their Megachurch services. These services have been raised, beyond Martin Heidegger's *Sacred Space*[19] to the level of a Las Vegas production. Can you imagine Jesus hosting a sing-along with rock bands doing bible songs? While I applaud valuable charitable services given through Christian organizations, I do not think financial charity reflects the actual teachings of Jesus. Financial generosity is not the kind of generosity Jesus taught. Jesus didn't want people to give their money to a church conglomerate. He wanted them to give of themselves to their neighbors, to participate with others in the Kingdom of Heaven on a one to one basis.

Jesus demanded personal involvement in a community of brother and sisterhood. Jesus seems to be a mixture of a "communalist" and "universalist." Just look at the story of the Good Samaritan, or the saying of John the Baptist who taught "He that hath two coats, let him impart to him that hath none." (Luke 3:11) Jesus also warns against greed and lack of sharing in the parable of the rich fool. He advises the honorable rich man to sell all his possessions and give to the poor. Treasure in heaven will be his reward. Now think of the high Christian clergy, who wear their expensive vestments and fancy shoes. They hoard gold and precious works of art, while poor people starve. Jesus talked about the birds of the air and the flowers in the fields. Did they not hear him? (Matthew 6:26-28) If money is so evil, perhaps Jesus should have added, "Woe to the church leaders who take money from the rich and the poor, they are tainted by their greed." It's hilarious, the churches aren't willing to give up their treasures, but they are happy to take yours.

Here is a fun vision I have of Jesus. He greets the well known Christian ministers as they arrive at the pearly gates. You know them well. They are on TV, Radio, and the Internet, always telling you they know what Jesus expects of you. At the same time, they spread the Good News; they are also willing to put your money to good use, building their kingdom on the earth, not the Kingdom of Heaven. Please show me the passages in the New Testament where Jesus says, "Give me your money! Or, "Build great cathedrals in my name." I think Jesus would see this as an abomination compared to his life and teachings. My feeling is this is just one reason Jesus said while dying on the cross, "Father, forgive them; for they know not what they do." (Luke 23:34) They turned Jesus into a money-making machine.

Imagine this scene in your mind. One of these preachers passes away and heads up to heaven. He may take his jet to get there. He arrives at the pearly gates and is ecstatic when he sees Jesus standing there with open arms. He says, "Jesus . . . ! Oh, Jesus! I am humbled and proud you are here to welcome me into heaven with open arms.

I have worked all my life spreading your Good News to others. I have saved many souls by telling them your story and leading them to your salvation. Oh, Jesus! Oh, Jesus!" At this point, Jesus, who is still standing there with arms stretched out in front of his body, palms slightly raised, begins to speak. He says, "No (fill in the name of the preacher) you've got it all wrong. I am not welcoming you with open arms. I want to know, where is all the money you took from others in my name? Give it to me now!" Here is an exciting project for you. Go to Google and search the gross worth (and I do mean gross) of the most popular Christian ministers. You may be surprised at the results.

I have another vision of Jesus as he comes back to earth. He arrives at the Vatican, looking for the pope. He is dressed in everyday clothes and approaches the door to the pope's private quarters. The Swiss Guard confront and question him. They want to know what he thinks he is doing coming to the pope's quarters without an invitation. Jesus was rarely if ever intimidated and tells the guards; he wants to see the pope. The guards, not knowing who he is, and influenced by his average appearance, tells him he can't. Jesus undaunted says, "You don't know who I AM! I want to see the pope now!" The guards refuse and tell him to go away. When he persists, they warn him he will be arrested if he continues to create a disturbance. But he again demands to see the pope, and still, the guards refuse. Once more Jesus questions why he cannot see the pope, the leader of "His" church. Frustrated by his unyielding approach, one of the guards replies, only special people can see the pope. You need an appointment, and besides, the pope isn't even here. He is at his summer residence in Lake Como.

How did the teachings and example of Jesus become so perverted? Fyodor Dostoyevsky's *The Grand Inquisitor*[20] paints a picture of what might have happened if Jesus had returned during the Inquisition. You may find it an enlightening read.

WHO DID JESUS HATE?

Whoa! You may say. Jesus is love incarnate. He didn't hate anyone. After a moment's consideration, you might say, "Well, I suppose Jesus hated sinners." That is untrue. He came to save them.

(1 Timothy 1:15) After a more profound reflection, you might say, "Ah! I know, Jesus hated the Scribes, Pharisees, Priests, and leaders of the people. Read Matthew 23 and Luke 11 for an explicit tirade against them. They are surely the ones he hated." Some might say, "Jesus hated the Jewish Nation, who rejected him and killed him. Didn't he curse the Jewish Nation in the story of the withered fig tree (one of the symbols of the Jews)? He also predicted the destruction of the Temple." But, I say, "Wait a moment. Did you notice no one blames the Romans?" In the trial scene before Pilate, the New Testament writers give Pilate the perfect out. He washes his hands of the whole matter. History doesn't always lie, although the writers of the New Testament surely stretch the truth. Jesus was brutally tortured and killed by the Romans. The leaders of the Jews, who collaborated with Rome, may have handed Jesus over to them, but they did not kill him. The Jews were ruled harshly and overtaxed by the Romans. The Jews hated their oppressors and revolted against them. Shouldn't the Romans be attacked in the New Testament for all their injustices? Jesus says, "Render to Caesar the things that are Caesar's, and to God the things that are God's." (Mark 12:17) I always thought this was a bit odd, isn't everything God's?

Lets us consider the purpose of the life of Jesus. He tells us, "For the Son of man has come to save that which was lost." (Matthew 18:11) Oops! Sorry, that line has been left out or changed in newer versions of the New Testament. Scholars felt that it was a poor copy of Luke 19:10, which reads, "To seek and to save that which was lost." Jesus says, "I came not to call the righteous, but sinners to repentance." (Mark 2:17) But Jesus also said he did not come to bring peace, but rather a sword.

Is his purpose to bring peace or a sword? It cannot be both. He judges the Scribes and Pharisees as sinners using some offensive language. Why didn't he call them to salvation? Instead, he condemned them. He was a sword against them. This condemnation appears to be a contradiction of his mission. Doesn't Jesus come to save all God's children, and especially sinners? Here is a more stunning contradiction. Mark 4:10-11, Matthew 13:10-13, and Luke

8: 9-10 suggest the Apostles received private or "secret" teachings from Jesus. However, Jesus directly contradicts this by saying, "In secret, I have said nothing." (John 18:20) How can Jesus make this statement?

Jesus had no reason to lie. He knew what his enemies were planning. Scholars suggest political and social reasons are behind these contradictions. They point out; the original Jesus movement was a Jewish movement. It was competing with other Jewish groups of the day. Perhaps these were not the words of Jesus, but words put in his mouth by members of the early Jesus movement. Part of their purpose was to refute the "Gnostic Gospels" floating around during this time. The word "Gnostic" comes from "gnosis" and means knowledge. The early Jesus movement may have been refuting other theories or teachings. The problem becomes enormous when seen in the context of "truth." The Gospel According to John stretches the truth in this instance for political or competitive reasons. So we must ask, what other "manufactured truths" may be in the New Testament?

Look at the history of Christianity; there were plenty of competing movements. Ever hear of heresy? Heresy can be a contrary opinion concerning a doctrine. Competing movements existed in early Christianity and still do to this day. The world seems to have plenty of angry Christians. How can that be? What would Jesus think about the way his life and teachings are used and presented to the people? I am sure it causes him great suffering, "Forgive them, Father!"

THE SCRIBES AND PHARISEES

Who were the Scribes and Pharisees, and why did Jesus rebuke and hate them? Did He? The Pharisees were a Jewish sect. Some of the Scribes Jesus interacted with were probably members of it. Historians tell us the Pharisees came to influence after the death of Jesus. If this is true, they could not be the target of his arrows, but rather those of his early followers, who were competing with the Scribes and Pharisees. The Scribes knew Jewish Law or the Law of Moses. Their job was to study, interpret, and comment on the Law, both in oral and written terms. They played an essential structural and religious role, guiding a society that lived by the Law of Moses. They lived at a time when their community faced threats, not only from outside Roman influence but also from disruptive forces from within. They were instrumental in setting up the cultural rules by which the Jewish People lived. Scholars suggest that without them, we probably would not have the insight into the Jewish teachings we have today. The Jewish people were the original people known as the People of the Book. It is partially due to the efforts of the Scribes.

There are several reasons problems existed between the Pharisees, Scribes, Jewish leaders, and Jesus. One rested on the interpretation and legalism placed on the Law by them. They added regulations and traditions that seemed to be more compelling than the Law itself, or the "Spirit of the Law." It appears that happened all over again, with the advent of mainstream Christianity. Another was the competition for the hearts and minds of the Jews of the time, between the early Jesus movement, other contemporary movements, and the fractionalized Jewish society, which was under grave stress. Biblical scholars note, the Jesus movement was a Jewish movement, not a Christian movement. There were also other movements at the time.

Ever hear of the Essenes, Qumran, and the Dead Sea Scrolls? The Christian movement we know today developed later and grew among the Gentiles, primarily through the influence of Paul. Jesus was more interested in the "Spirit of the Law" not the legalism of it. The Scribes and Pharisees knew the Law and told others how to live by it. However, according to Jesus, they did not live up to it themselves. Just think of the politicians who do this to each other and us every day, and you can understand the problems associated with living in a fractionalized and stressed society. Now consider the voluminous writings of Christian Scribes, (scholars, priests, and theologians) who over the ages have made the legalism of the Jewish Scribes and Pharisees look like "kid's stuff." But let us move on to more salient issues.

THE LAST SUPPER

Jesus enters Jerusalem in a victorious procession with crowds of people singing, throwing their coats on the ground, and waving palms. If you are the oppressor of the city, the Romans, you would have noticed this. After the triumphant arrival in Jerusalem, he cleanses the Temple, creating an uproar. If you are the oppressor of the city, the Romans, you would have noticed this also. If you are the oppressor of the city, the Romans, and you heard Jesus say, "Think not that I am come to send peace on earth: I came not to send peace, but a sword." (Matthew 10:34) What would you think of Jesus and his followers? The Romans had a history of being cruel oppressors; they would take notice. They used spies and collaborators to keep a heavy hand on social unrest. They knew an important Jewish holy day was approaching, and the Jews had a reputation for creating unrest. If the Romans stopped trouble before it gained momentum, they saved themselves a lot of anguish later. It is easy to speculate the Romans were aware Jesus was in Jerusalem. If a sword were coming to Jerusalem, they would be ready to crush it with swift and violent means.

Jesus hosted the Last Supper. Like Heidegger's concept of "sacred space," Mircea Eliade explains the idea of "participation" in *Myths, Dreams, and Mysteries*[21]. Just as we can enter a sacred space, we can participate in a sacred ceremony. Catholicism teaches we partake in the mystery of the Last Supper by sharing in the Eucharist. However, it is important to understand Jesus hosted the Last Supper as an extraordinary occasion. I do not think he envisioned this event would become the equivalent of the daily news on TV.

Several important events occur during the Last Supper. Among them are the following: the symbolic sharing and teaching of the bread and wine, the announcement he would be betrayed by one of his own, the prediction of Peter's denial, and the dispute over who would be the greatest among the Apostles. The Gospel of John adds even more with the "Upper Room Discourse." The other Gospel writers seem to have forgotten about this, and some of the promises made in John. But in my understanding, something more significant occurred at the Last Supper. It was the washing of the feet, an act of humility. Doesn't this fit the mission of Jesus more than the brutality of the bread and wine? This is my body; this is my blood! The washing of the feet does not focus on guilt, but rather on humility, service, and love. This act became more meaningful when Jesus made an example of Peter's refusal.

The entrance into Jerusalem and the Last Supper are a pivotal point in the New Testament. They separate the earlier teaching portion of the life of Jesus and introduce us to the Passion of Jesus. His teachings give us valuable information concerning how Jesus wanted us to live. In esoteric terms, Jesus is the quintessential representative of the Age of Pisces. The symbol of the fish even represents him, and his first disciples were fishermen. Two fish represent the Astrological sign of Pisces. Each swim in a different direction. Like the Yin and Yang symbol of the Tao, they show the duality of nature fluctuating in a complementary and interconnected balance. Pisces is also the sign associated with spirituality, compassion, sacrifice, and wisdom. Another correspondence is the sign's rulership of the feet. Could it be, the more substantial teaching given by Jesus was the example of humility, by washing the feet of the Apostles? The body and blood sacrifice put the focus on the suffering of Jesus above all else. It became the central theme in Christianity. "Repent! Jesus suffered and died for your sins!"

This focus can even be witnessed in the beautifully simple Hail Mary prayer, central to Mariology in the Catholic Church. Initially, a simple prayer, it recounted the greeting of the Archangel Gabriel to the Virgin Mary in the Gospel of Luke. "Hail, thou that art highly favoured, the Lord is with thee: blessed art thou among women." (Luke 1:28) But even the beautiful words of the Angel Gabriel could not survive the Scribes and Pharisees of the Catholic Church. A line was added in 1555 by St. Petrus Canisius, and officially adopted at the Council of Trent. Here are the new words; they speak for themselves "Holy Mary, Mother of God, **pray for us sinners.**" Think about it! If there are no sinners, there is no need for the church conglomerate. At the Last Supper, several events take place. Jesus' washing the feet of the disciples was the first on the agenda. (John 13:1-20) During the meal, Jesus spoke of the betrayer. (Mark 14:17-21, Matthew

26:20-25, Luke 22:21-23) The meal seems to have included some of the traditional Passover elements. Also, even though John gives us a different night for the meal than the synoptic writers, the commencement of the Lord's Supper, with words the disciples had probably never heard at a Passover meal. (Luke 22:19-20) John's Gospel avoids giving us yet another description of this ceremony. His omission is surprising since the sharing of the bread and wine is the centerpiece of the Christian mass. Unlike the other gospel writers, he includes the "Upper Room Discourse, an extensive message. (John 14-17) It concludes with Jesus' "High Priestly Prayer" of intercession for his followers. Scholars suggest, it may have been prayed during mealtime, or perhaps later. There is a significant promise made by Jesus in this discourse; I will address it later. The Synoptic Gospels (Mark, Matthew, and Luke) report the disciples' argument about who would be the greatest, along with the response by Jesus. (Luke 22:24-30) Jesus also addresses the overconfident Peter about his future denial (Luke 22:31-34), and then his words about being prepared to face a hostile world. (John 15-16) The supper ends with a hymn, and they depart to the Garden of Gethsemane. Jesus opened his heart in prayer there, with little support from the disciples. (Luke 22:39-46) Jesus will be arrested and handed over for trial and execution.

Light from Water

Thomas F. Kearns

CHAPTER 5 - FOUR PATHS TO PASSION
(LATIN: PASSIONEM - SUFFERING, ENDURING)

Most people today would not use the word passion to describe suffering. However, this is the way it is used to describe the last few days of Jesus' life. As in other parts of the Gospels, there are differences in the telling. Three descriptions in the Synoptic Gospels and a separate one in John. Again, I strongly suggest you read the work of Bible historian, Bart D. Ehrman. His extensive knowledge and a clear grasp of the language and events of the "Passion" will give you new insight. He also suggests an effective way of studying the New Testament. It will allow you to see the differences and contradictions for yourself. I will use a different method later to demonstrate them.

Many historians suggest Mark's Gospel came first, approximately 40 years or so after the death of Jesus. It is followed by Matthew and Luke, about 55 - 60 years after the death of Jesus, and then John's Gospel written approximately 60 - 80 years after the death of Jesus. It is essential to understand and consider the following: there are no original copies of the Gospels; no one knows for sure who the Gospel authors were, it is a topic of debate; and the Gospels were written in Greek, not Aramaic, which was the language spoken by Jesus. The stories are based on oral traditions, which had been shared by everyday

Light from Water

people over decades. The earliest copy known is a fragment of John's Gospel called P52. It is about 3 x 2 inches and dated to about 120 years after the death of Jesus. It is more than possible; many changes were made in the stories, which calls their integrity into question. Scholars debate these issues among themselves, and you can listen to some of these interesting debates on YouTube.

Christians know the story of the Passion of Jesus, but perhaps not as well as they think. I surely did not, until I researched and studied them as suggested by Ehrman. After the Last Supper, Jesus goes to the garden to pray. He asks his apostles to watch with him, but they fall asleep after a while. He is disappointed by them, a theme seen throughout the Gospels. Also, in my opinion, an indication of what will occur throughout the history of Christianity. It continues to this day. The betrayal by Judas could be a sign of things to come. Jesus would probably be very disappointed in his namesake religion. It seems to have betrayed his teachings. A few unusual things take place when the soldiers of the High Priest come to arrest him. One of the apostles pulls a sword and cuts off the ear of a servant of the High Priest. In Mark, Jesus says little about this. (Mark 14:47) Matthew has Jesus say, "Put up again thy sword into his place: for all they that take up the sword shall perish with the sword." (Matthew 26:52) (Didn't Jesus say he came to be a sword?) But only in Luke it reads, "Suffer ye thus far. And he touched his ear, and healed him." (Luke 22:51) How did the other writers miss this miracle? John tells us it is Peter who cuts off the servant's ear. We find out the servant's name is Malchus. (John 18:10-11) Jesus identifies himself to the mob. They went backward and fell to the ground. This event is only in John. (18:6) How did the Synoptic Gospel writers miss the mob falling to the ground? That is pretty impressive!

Jesus comes before the High Priest who asks him, "Art thou the Christ, the Son of the Blessed?" Jesus answers, "I am: and ye shall see the Son of man sitting on the right hand of power, and coming in the clouds of heaven." (Mark 14:62) This statement is repeated a bit differently in each of the Synoptic Gospels, but John does not mention it. The High Priest says this is blasphemy. As this is going on, Peter is warming himself by the fire and denies knowing Jesus three times as predicted. Since the Jews do not have the power to execute Jesus, they must bring him before Pilate. Here we encounter several different details from each author. In Mark (15) and Matthew (27), Jesus is taken to Pilate. In John, the Jews did not follow. (18:28) If John is correct, how do we know any of the details of what happened to Jesus? The conversation between Jesus and Pilate happens without the Jews being present. Perhaps one of the most damaging lines in the New Testament occurs when Pilate doesn't want to condemn Jesus. The Jews tell him, "His blood be on us, and on our children." (Matthew 27:25) You should read Thomas Sheehan's book *The First Coming*[22] for the effect this line had on the Jewish people if you cannot figure it out for yourself. Even if some of the Jewish leaders were complicit in the death of Jesus, the Jewish people did not kill Jesus. The Romans did! But because of the way the story tells it, we can hate and kill the Jews. We can also take their property, as was done in Alexandria by Bishop Cyril. History proves the attitude inspired by this onerous line goes way beyond this abuse. I would argue, this and other statements, set up a philosophy of hatred against anyone who would refute Christian Theology. How can a Christian hate anyone? Here is another question. Who was there to witness Pilate's wife's message about her dream? (Matthew 27:19) Why does only one author talk about Jesus going to Herod? (Luke 23: 6-12) Did the other writers not witness this, or hear about it? And how does the author know Herod and Pilate became friends on that day? A fascinating and highly unlikely statement.

    Parts of the Passion of Jesus story are told vividly in the "Stations of the Cross." As a child, and in my teen years, I participated in the Stations many times. It includes some events not found in the Gospels at all. Its focus on the suffering and humiliation of Jesus makes it a compelling narrative. I do not mean to disregard, or in any way, diminish the pain of Jesus. However, the Stations demonstrate once again the focus Christianity has put on his suffering, more than on his glory. I am sure Christians would say his suffering is his glory, or at least an essential part of it. I feel it has been used to control believers, and influence guilt and fear in them. This influence also occurs in Holy Communion. Imagine being a small child, having to eat the body and blood of Jesus. "Don't chew the host!" The nuns prepared us well for the sacred event.

There is another questionable contradiction in this story. In the Synoptic Gospels, Jesus, brutalized by the Romans, is too weak to carry his cross, a normal part of this Roman torture. A man from the country, a passerby, Simon of Cyrene is made to bear the cross for him. Interestingly, the Gospel of John contradicts this and says Jesus carried the cross himself. "And he bearing his cross went forth into a place called the place of a skull, which is called in the Hebrew Golgotha:" (John 19:17) Perhaps John wanted to show there was no weakness in Jesus. How could the savior of the world show weakness? Even though the Romans brutalized him, he still carried his cross. Luke also adds a multitude of people following the procession, and the Daughters of Jerusalem line, which prophesied the suffering of the Jews, the destruction of the Temple, and Jerusalem. These additions suggest these future events will be retribution against the Jews for rejecting and killing Jesus.

SEVEN LAST WORDS OF THE CRUCIFIED JESUS

There are seven phrases that Jesus says while he is dying on the cross. They are: "Eloi, Eloi, lama sabachthani? which is, being interpreted, My God, my God, why hast thou forsaken me?" (Mark 15:34 and Matthew 27:46)

"Then said Jesus, Father, forgive them; for they know not what they do." (Luke 23:34)

"And Jesus said unto him, Verily I say unto thee, Today shalt thou be with me in paradise." (Luke 23:43)

"Father, into thy hands I commend My spirit:" (Luke 23:46)

"Woman, behold thy son!" "Then saith he to the disciple, Behold thy mother!" (John 19:26-27)

"I thirst." (John 19:28)

"It is finished:" (John 19:30)

Jesus had predicted his suffering and death on many occasions in the New Testament. Roman Soldiers, experts in brutality, oppressors in a conquered land delivered his torture. They knew how to hurt someone very badly, yet still, keep them barely alive so that they could suffer more. Jesus was so debilitated; he could not carry his cross (except in John). Then he was further brutalized by soldiers nailing his hands and feet to the cross. It is almost impossible to picture him crying out in a loud voice, so people at a distance could hear what he was saying. John tells us, his mother, and his mother's sister Mary, the wife of Cleophas, and Mary Magdalene were standing by the cross but makes no mention of the Beloved Disciple. Where did he go? Where would Jesus get the strength to speak? Also, it is highly unlikely the Roman soldiers would allow a crowd to hang out at the foot of the cross. Luke tells us his followers stood afar. "And all his acquaintance and the women that followed him from Galilee stood afar off, beholding these things." (Luke 23:49) If Luke is correct, who was the witness to his words? The Roman soldiers? Would they report them to the Jewish followers of Jesus? Unlikely! If Jesus freely accepted the role of the savior of the world, and he says he does in the Garden (Thy will be done), why would he ever feel forsaken by God? Isn't he God? (Eloi, Eloi, lama sabachthani?) Read the introduction of Psalm 22 in the Old Testament. It is probably being used to connect Jesus to the Psalms, as proof of past prophecies. Or, if Jesus said this, what did he expect God to do? Miraculously take him down from the cross, and bring him to glory? Perhaps, we can only wonder.

    Jesus also says, "Father, forgive them; for they know not what they do." (Luke 23:34) These words demonstrate the depth of forgiveness in Jesus. The soldiers are killing him; they have tortured him; they are casting lots for his clothes; he forgives them. Who could be that forgiving? Could he have had something else in mind? As I mentioned above, Jesus made many prophesies in the New Testament. The ones about his death are an essential theme. There are others concerning the future of Judea (the withered fig tree and the Destruction of the Temple). Jesus also predicted the denials by Peter. I feel the "forgive them" plea (Luke 23:34), has nothing to do with what was happening at the moment. It represents another form of a prediction. Jesus is looking into the future, seeing the outcome of his teachings, and the actions his followers will take in his name. He is seeing how Christianity will institutionalize his life and death and use him for its chosen plans. Creating not the Kingdom of Heaven, but its kingdom on earth. Perhaps, he also saw the many brutalities that occurred under his banner. A little investigation on Google will give you a very long list of atrocities perpetrated by Christianity. You will find, war, killing, torture, and most sadly, the little children who will be harmed by the "Scribes" and "Pharisees" of the religion named after him. I have personal experience in this regard. Do not think the children have been victimized only in our time. This brutality has probably gone on for centuries. Can you imagine dying for that? It truly broke his heart. It truly gave him unbearable suffering.

Jesus had an unlikely short conversation with one of the two other men crucified with him. (Luke 23: 39-43) We do not know what their crimes were, but supposedly one of them was mocking Jesus — telling him to save them and himself if he was indeed the Messiah. The other defended Jesus, rebuking the first criminal saying, "Dost not thou fear God, seeing thou art in the same condemnation? And we indeed justly; for we receive the due reward of our deeds: but this man hath done nothing amiss." (Luke 23: 40-41) How did a criminal know that? After saying this, he turns to Jesus and asks to be remembered when Jesus enters his kingdom. Jesus answers him, saying, "Verily I say unto thee, Today shalt thou be with me in paradise." (Interesting how dying, brutally tortured men, hanging from crosses on the brink of death, could have a conversation.) Even Christian teaching refutes the paradise idea. Jesus did not go directly to paradise. He went to Hades to free the souls trapped there. They were waiting for him to open the doors of heaven to the good souls. They could not get into heaven until his death and resurrection. Another question arises about this conversation. Remember, if Luke is correct, the acquaintances of Jesus and the women who followed him from Galilee, stood "afar off," (Luke 23: 49) How did they hear what a crucified, brutalized, suffering and dying man was saying? Was he shouting it out?

The line in Luke that Jesus says just as he dies, "Father, into thy hands I commend my spirit:" (Luke 23:46) makes sense, as do the lines in John 19 "I thirst" and "It is finished." If Jesus was expecting some miraculous event (Eloi, Eloi, lama sabachthani?), to intervene in his suffering and death, it did not happen. We did not see the Son of man coming with the clouds and Angels of Heaven, and we still have not to this day. His life was finished. An interesting event occurs, "And the graves were opened; and many bodies of the saints which slept arose, and came out of the graves after his resurrection, and went into the holy city, and appeared unto many." (Matthew 27:52-53) No other writer reported this miracle, neither a disciple of Jesus nor a historian. You would think such an event would stand out. After Jesus rose from the dead, why didn't he visit the Scribes and Pharisees? That would have been a coup and convinced them! They would have converted the people and saved many more souls. Just think, if Jesus appeared to Pilate, Christianity might have won over the whole Roman Empire without all the suffering and torture.

There is another extraordinary line that occurs in John. It is said to Mary and the Beloved Disciple (No one seems to know who that was). "Woman, behold thy son!" Then He said to the disciple, "Behold thy mother!" (John 19:26-27) The disciples of Jesus had vanished at his arrest and were probably hiding in fear of their deaths. Mary might be at the Crucifixion, but it is highly unlikely any of his disciples would be near. The Gospels tell us, Jesus was taken down from the cross to be buried. Historians suggest this would be unlikely. The purpose of crucifixion was to shame and humiliate the victim, allowing the tortured naked body to deteriorate in public. Rome used the spectacle to drive fear into the hearts of his followers, or other enemies, who would stir up trouble. There are few reports of the Romans ever allowing the body of a revolutionary to be taken down from the cross and buried. But this act was needed in Christianity because Jesus would rise from the dead. The story writers knew he needed to be in a tomb to do so.

THE TOMB

The death of Jesus was horrific. But in terms of Christian belief, a necessary evil. However, the Resurrection of Jesus was critically important. If there was no Resurrection, all the suffering of Jesus was for naught, and there is no Christianity. Not that there was supposed to be. So who were the witnesses to this earth changing event?

Most people have grown up on television programs and videos. They tend to understand in a visual sense more than by reading. I will use the mass media format so you can easily visualize the most critical part of the New Testament: the Resurrection. If Jesus does not rise from the dead, the Jesus movement in Judaism dies. If the Jesus movement dies, Paul will not have the opportunity to transform it into what would become Christianity.

Imagine yourself as the producer and director of a film project. You have solicited rough scripts from four different writers. Now you must decide which script you will use to tell the story the way you want to portray it — first some background. There are no eyewitnesses to this story. The guards placed outside the tomb were paid off to say his followers stole the body of Jesus, or the event froze them with fear. The followers of Jesus were not present at the Resurrection. They cannot be considered eyewitnesses. However, we can take their testimony and see what we can glean from their reports. Many movies have been made about the Bible and the life and death of Jesus. The process of rough sketching a film or television script will help you visualize the story. Now we must evaluate the scripts. Here is how they read.

MARK
Scene one: The tomb of Jesus:
The cast: Mary Magdalena, Mary, the Mother of Jesus, and Salome.
The action: Three women are coming to the tomb to anoint the body of Jesus. They're wondering how they are going to get into the tomb blocked by a large stone.

Scene two: In the tomb:
The cast: The tomb is open. A man in the long white robe is in the

tomb. He addresses the women.
The action: He tells them not to be frightened and to tell the apostles Jesus has risen.
They are frightened and run away. The women tell no one.

MATTHEW
Scene one: The tomb of Jesus:
The cast: Mary Magdalena and the other Mary.
The action: They arrive at the tomb.

Scene two: In the tomb:
The cast: Jesus, an Angel of the Lord, and the women.
The action: A great earthquake occurs, and the large stone is moved opening the tomb. An Angel of the Lord sits upon the stone. The guards have become like stone. The Angel says fear not, he has risen. Go tell his disciples he will meet them in Galilee.

Scene three: On the Road:
The cast: Jesus, Mary Magdalena, and the other Mary.
The action: The women run to tell the disciples. On the way, they meet Jesus. They hold him by his feet and worshiped him.

LUKE
Scene one: The tomb of Jesus:
The cast: Mary Magdalene, Joanna, Mary, the Mother of Jesus, and other women from Galilee arrive.

Scene two: In the tomb:
The cast: Two men in shining garments and the women.
The action: The women come to the tomb to anoint the body of Jesus. The body of Jesus is not there. Two men in shining garments tell them, he has risen.

Scene three: The women return to the Apostles.
The action: The women tell the Apostles what they saw, but the

apostles do not believe them.
    Scene four: Peter runs to the tomb.
    The action: He wonders what happened.

JOHN
Scene one: The tomb of Jesus:
The cast: Mary Magdalene
The action: Mary goes to the tomb, finds it open and runs to tell Simon Peter.

    Scene two: Peter and the other disciple.
    The action: They run to the tomb and find it empty.

    Scene three: Outside the tomb:
    The cast: Jesus and Mary Magdalena.
    The action: Mary sees Jesus but does not recognize him. She thinks he is the gardener. She asks, where have they laid him? Jesus says her name, and she recognizes him. He tells her not to cling to him.

    Scene four: Jesus, Thomas, and the other disciples.
    The action: Jesus tells Thomas to put his hands in his wounds so he can believe.

    In Christian terms, the most momentous event in the history of the world is the Resurrection of Jesus. How can four authors, believers in Jesus, and these the most important words in history, tell this story and have such variations and contradictions? Just look them over carefully. The details of the narratives do not agree. Mary can touch Jesus in one script, yet she is warned not to in another. We have heard for centuries the Gospels are the "Good News" the Holy, Sacred Word of God. However, it is important to remember; these are also the words people have used as a license to kill people, scare people, annihilate nations, and abuse children. How could the words, examples, and teachings of Jesus ever be used to harm anyone?

Thomas F. Kearns

CRUCIFIXION OR RESURRECTION
PROMETHEUS BOUND

Christian writers tell us all of the conflicts of information and stories mentioned in the previous pages are well known to Christian Scholars and most Christian Ministers. They are taught and debated in Seminaries and Divinity Schools. You can see many of the debates on YouTube. However, even though most Christian Ministers know this information, you would rarely, hear them preach it to their congregations. They continue using the New Testament stories in the same old ways. They use them to put a price on Jesus and his followers. It is unfortunate. Let us look at the most critical and central issue in dealing with Christian teaching. How Jesus, his life, death, and teachings, have been portrayed to the world for two thousand years, and how his story is still used to influence individual lives and our culture.

There are many stories in the Old Testament that seem to be precursors to events in the New Testament. Scholars speculate they were used by early pre-Christian writers, to validate and legitimize the teachings of the New Testament. In other words, parts of the New Testament were written to fit the Old Testament narrative and predictions. Perhaps one of the most important, in my estimation, is called "The Binding of Isaac." It comes from Genesis 22 where God tells Abraham to sacrifice his son Isaac. It is important to note, that Isaac was the son promised to Abraham and Sarah from God in their old age, almost a miraculous birth. Just as Christians see Jesus, the promised Messiah, born through the Immaculate Conception, as a promised miraculous birth. Isaac was very precious to Abraham and Sarah. God wanted to test the obedience of Abraham, so he tells him to sacrifice Isaac, to kill him with his own hands. Child sacrifice occurred in ancient times, but this child, Isaac, was a gift from God.

Wouldn't an all-knowing God already "know" if Abraham was going to be obedient? Why the need for a blood sacrifice? Does God want Abraham to prove his obedience to God, to himself? Abraham, following God's order, brings Isaac to Mount Moriah and prepares to kill him. He is interrupted dramatically at the last moment by the

Angel of the Lord. He sees a ram caught in a thicket, and following the instruction of the Angel, kills it instead. The story sets the stage for the later sacrifice of Jesus. However, even though Jesus asks that this cup be taken from him, and he may be looking for a Divine intervention, God does not spare him. He becomes the sacrifice. Looking at the Passion of Jesus, it is clear Jesus was not completely happy about what was to happen. He asked for intervention. However, he complied. "And he said, Abba, Father, all things are possible unto thee; take away this cup from me: nevertheless not what I will, but what thou wilt." (Mark 14:36, Matthew 26:39, Luke 22:42)

A FEW QUESTIONS FOR YOU TO CONSIDER

1) If God could spare Isaac, why couldn't Jesus be spared? He asked to have this cup taken from him.

2) If Christians love Jesus so much, why won't they spare him? Why won't they set him free? Why do they continue to sacrifice him?

3) Why the need for a human/god sacrifice? Couldn't the all-loving, all-forgiving, Almighty God have said, "You're forgiven!"

4) Why was God feeling guilty about all the suffering in the world? Didn't He create the world the way it is?

5) Why was the most difficult and lowest point of Jesus' life (the Crucifixion) elevated to the highest?

6) Why did Christianity take the highest pinnacle of his life, the Resurrection, and Ascension, and diminish them, by pushing them into the background? If you think they didn't, visit a Christian Church. Count and compare the number of crosses and crucifixes, to Resurrection and Ascension scenes. "And Jesus answered them, saying, The hour is come, that the Son of man should be glorified." (John 12:23)

7) Do Christians glorify Jesus, or do they stigmatize him?

8) Why did the theocracy and dogma of the Church become more important than the teachings of Jesus? This is the opposite of what Jesus taught, and why he attacked the religious structure (Scribes and Pharisees) of his time.

9) Why were the people most important to Jesus, but least important to the Christian Church?

JESUS THE ARCHETYPE

Anyone familiar with the work of *Carl Gustav Jung*[23] will recognize how Jesus fits the archetype of the hero in his theory of the collective unconscious. He may also be the best example of *Joseph Campbell's Monomyth*[24]. His life plays out many of its essential themes. Most importantly, the great boon he brings to the world is eternal salvation. Not many heroes, in any mythology, did that! It is such a universal boon; he easily supersedes Prometheus, who merely brings fire to a cold, suffering humanity. But even Prometheus had a hero, Heracles who freed him.

Jesus also makes a double move and conquers time. He travels to Hades to free the souls waiting since the creation of humankind and original sin. Therefore, this is a genuinely magnificent boon, not just to current humanity, but to all souls. He frees them from the darkness of the eternal loss of God. He opens the doors of Hades, so the good souls, who were there, by no fault of their own, having lost the presence of God, can be reunited with eternal bliss. There are many papers and books written concerning the subject of myths and religious archetypes, so I will not go into that subject here. You can merely seek them out through a Google search, and the mystic psychology of it, psychic (soul) – ology (knowledge), will be made present to you. The problem with Jesus being the archetype of the hero and savior is the images of his role will eternally burn in the consciousness of the collective. If you believe in the eternal nature of the soul, Jesus will never be set free. Christianity will foster his suffering forever, or as long as humanity exists. Who will be the hero for Jesus?

THE BODY AND BLOOD

Most Christians see the mass ritual of the bread and wine, as an essential part of honoring Jesus and participating in the sacred feast. It is the main symbolic and miraculous vessel of Christianity, allowing the simple bread and wine to become the sacred body and blood of Christ. This symbolic sacrifice is played out in thousands of churches, thousands of times each day. Jesus merely did it once, as a special occasion. It puts the focus on the suffering and death of Jesus. It reminds each Christian, God was willing to sacrifice his only begotten son to save you. God allowed Jesus to be humiliated and sacrificed for your sins. Combined with the brutalized body of Jesus hanging over most Christian altars or at least the cross, it conveys a message empowered by a tremendous feeling of guilt. Jesus died for your sins!

Here is the prayer you repeat as you receive Holy Communion. Imagine saying this every day as a child, "Lord, I am not worthy that you should enter under my roof, but only say the word, and my soul shall be healed." I can't imagine how many times Christians encounter the brutalized body of Jesus on the crucifix. Think of the millions of times, over thousands of years. It can have an especially powerful effect on the young, the most vulnerable to Christian, or any propaganda. I remember being afraid of hurting Jesus when I first received Holy Communion. "Don't chew on the host! Jesus died for your sins! Be good, or you will not be saved! You will burn in hell forever!" Thankfully, they at least covered his body up a bit - the Romans didn't. It would be wonderful if they would set him free and stop brutalizing him.

THE CRUCIFIX

Words and images have power. As a young Catholic, I was most aware of the crucifix, the symbol of Christianity. It was everywhere: in my home, bedroom, schoolroom, above the altar at church, in school offices and even in the library. We carried it with us; we wore it. Everywhere I went in church terms, the crucifix with the suffering, brutalized, dying, or dead body of Jesus was present. It reminded us of the great sacrifice for our sins and our guilt. Isn't it odd, this ubiquitous symbol used by Christians today, was not the original symbol used by the early Jewish, Pre-Christian movement? The early Jews and Gentiles who followed the teachings of Jesus before there was a Christianity, used various devices, symbols, or marks to represent their movement. These included the fish, the Alpha and Omega, the Tau-Rho (T over P), the Chi-Rho (P over X), the Good Shepherd, the dove with an olive branch, and a simple cross - but not the crucifix. The crucifix was established later as the main symbol of Christianity. I don't know who, when, or what idea, changed the early Christian sacred symbols to the crucifix, but it probably took a few hundred years for it to dominate. I can only imagine someone in the bureaucracy of the Church made the suffering of Jesus the focus because it had more emotional power. It also harmonized better with the idea we are all sinners, and Jesus suffered and died for our sins. It seems they overlooked something, Jesus taught love, forgiveness, and eternal salvation - not eternal guilt.

The sacrifice of Jesus is one of the central themes in Christian doctrine. However, the death of Jesus is meaningless, and I am not in any way denigrating the suffering of Jesus. It is meaningless in this way. If there is no death, there can be no Resurrection. No Resurrection, no Christianity - or at least there should not be. Look at the difference in the Word of Life Mural at Notre Dame (touchdown Jesus) which depicts the glorified Jesus, and the crucifix, which represents the brutalized Jesus. Why focus on the negative? Why not have a beautiful and glorious image of the glorified Jesus above each altar? He could be standing tall in glory, with his arms outstretched in welcome to everyone. Wouldn't that make more sense? Yes, you would think. The purveyors of religion had a different vision. They could have shown the Son of man coming through the clouds to set up a kingdom, as he said he would. (Mark 13:26, Matthew 24:30 and Luke 21:27) But could they? Two thousand years have passed. This vision and prophecy of Jesus have not happened. These are the words of Jesus, or are they? Don't they also reflect the vision of Daniel? (7:13)

You may think: Ah! But only the Father would know the day and time. It is pretty evident Jesus, as well as his followers, thought it would happen shortly. "That this generation shall not pass, till all these things be done." (Mark 13:30, Luke 21:32)

Beyond the synoptic passages, there is an interesting discourse between Jesus and Peter to reinforce the idea of a triumphant return.

It appears in John. It seems Peter is jealous of the Beloved Disciple. Jesus has just told Peter, he would have to suffer a similar death to his own. Peter asks, and what about him (referring to the Beloved Disciple)? Jesus replies, "If I will that he tarry till I come, what is that to thee? Follow thou me." (John 21:22) This statement by Jesus suggests he fully understood his victorious return would be soon and at least within the lifetime of the Beloved Disciple. How could Jesus be wrong?

I mentioned "Touch Down Jesus" at Notre Dame for a specific reason. Remember all the Christians who were tortured and martyred in the coliseum. Thankfully, physical torture is no longer a part of the public spectacles of today. However, here is a Catholic Institution making money on the suffering of young men, who destroy their bodies for fame, glory, and dollars for Notre Dame. Do you think Jesus would want to be associated with these modern games? I do not!

THE MATERIAL ROUTE

My teacher, Reverend Harry Bender, often said that men chose to take the material route over the spiritual route. Men became more involved in structuring a religion, rather than a way of living spiritually. Therefore, the newly developing Christian Church became something that would look very foreign to the vision of Jesus. As foreign as the many Christian TV stars who want to serve Jesus so much, they need your money to do so. Jesus, "And commanded them that they should take nothing for their journey, save a staff only; no scrip, no bread, no money in their purse:" when they went out to spread the Good News. (Mark 6:8, Matthew 10:9-10 and Luke 9:3)

Jesus walked among the people and rarely visited the impressive Temple in Jerusalem. The Jewish people might view the Temple in Jerusalem as Catholics would see the Vatican today. Yes, there are stories Jesus taught in the various synagogues in the small towns and villages, but they were probably primitive and simple places at best. Most of his interactions with the people and the Scribes and Pharisees happened in public places, not in lavish temples. The most memorable teachings of Jesus, like, "The Woman Taken in Adultery" or "The

Beatitudes" happened in the streets, or on a hillside. The manifestation of the early Jesus movement, the way Jesus lived and taught, became something different as Christianity developed. You should read Tom Harpur's book *For Christ's Sake*[24] to see if Jesus had any intention to start a religion. Would Jesus even recognize "His religion?" Perhaps not. This maybe one of the reasons why he said, "Father, forgive them; for they know not what they do." (Luke 23:34)

PROMISES NOT KEPT

The journey of humankind on the material path not only negated the teachings of Jesus but also denied the power of the promises made by Jesus. We can find these promises in the Gospel of John. They are quite powerful:

> Verily, verily, I say unto you, He that believeth on me, the works that I do shall he do also; and greater works than these shall he do; because I go unto my Father. And whatsoever ye shall ask in my name, that will I do, that the Father may be glorified in the Son. If ye shall ask any thing in my name, I will do it. (John 14:12-14)

There are millions of Christians who truly and deeply believe in Jesus. Of that, I have no doubt. However, if these promises made by Jesus were true, there would be a multitude of miracles happening in this world. There would also be world peace. There would be no need for hospitals. The miraculous powers promised would be evidenced every day in our lives. How many Christians have prayed in the name of Jesus for healing for themselves or someone they loved? How did they feel when their prayers went unanswered? How many believing Christians have walked on water? It has not occurred.

JESUS ON PRAYER

Jesus taught, "The Kingdom of God is at hand." (Mark 1:15, Matthew 3:2) His later followers put it into buildings and codified his teachings into a complex and confusing doctrine, which must be taken on faith because it defies logic. It also allowed them to collect a toll before you could "pass Go." Just think of the many prayers, masses, hymns, and chants said in Christian services that contradict the advice of Jesus. Jesus taught us to pray the simple and direct "Our Father." Jesus taught not to repeat prayers mindlessly. "But when ye pray, use not vain repetitions, as the heathen do: for they think that they shall be heard for their much speaking." (Matthew 6:7) Would Jesus ever accept praying to Mary or the Saints. It would be unthinkable, a blasphemy!

Simply put, the Christian bureaucracy pushed the people as far away from Jesus as possible. They made him a mystery and instituted a complex set of rules and teachings to shroud him from his followers. Christian theology has become a legalism that would inspire the Scribes and Pharisees, or "snakes and vipers" as Jesus referred to them. Unless of course, you believe Jesus, love and forgiveness incarnate according to Christianity, spoke the words in the woes. (Matthew 23:1-39)

Over the centuries, Christianity has evolved. It moved further away from Jesus as it incorporated into the Empire. It began with the conversion of Constantine. A vision told him to fight and kill his enemies under the sign of the cross. Isn't that a contradiction to loving your enemies, and turning the other cheek? His victory, and the Council of Nicaea in 325, totally changed the religion of Jesus, from a spiritual mission and way of life, into a codified complex bureaucracy filled and guided over the ages with what Jesus referred to as "whited sepulchers." (Matthew 23:27) Is it surprising Christianity has created so much suffering in the world? Is it surprising that Jesus had to say, "Father, forgive them; for they know not what they do." (Luke 23:34)

Every belief system needs a focus. The focus of Christianity changed from a beautifully simple life of loving God and your fellow man and woman, complete with a simple symbolic language, to an extravagant expression that used an almost abhorrent image to inspire "Fear and Trembling." You can still hear the promise; you will burn in hell if you don't accept Jesus! Jesus suffered and died for your sins on the cross! Wasn't it supposed to be, "Jesus loves you?" Think of the powerful and destructive effect this propaganda had on little children. Although its origin is disputed, Ignatius of Loyola reportedly said, "Give me the child for the first seven years, and I will give you the man." It has been the way of the Church for centuries. Church leaders and teachers instilled their propaganda into the hearts and minds of little children who had no defense. I am not suggesting everything taught was without worth, for that would not be accurate. But the object, purpose, and method can be questioned. Think of the little children who were brutalized by Christianity. Jesus wanted them to come to him in love and gentleness. Do you think the priest scandals of the past few decades is something new? I think not.

Light from Water

Thomas F. Kearns

CHAPTER 6 - THE POWER OF AN IMAGE

You can see the difference between the image of the Buddha, sitting in tranquility on the Lotus Flower, and the crucifix with the brutalized body of Jesus. Millions of people over thousands of years, have been killed and tortured by people of various religions who believe in the one true God. They killed in the name of God! I cannot repeat it too many times; if God wanted you dead, you'd be dead! God would not need any help.

Jesus continues to suffer from all the injustice rendered in his name. He is still impaled on the crucifix. Who can free Jesus from this torture and heavy karma? Who can be the Hero for Jesus? Who will save Jesus? Heracles freed Prometheus. But only two entities can do this mighty deed for Jesus. First, Jesus can free himself by the arrival of the Second Coming promised so long ago. Since it did not occur before "this generation has tasted death," it is unlikely to happen now. Who else could free Jesus? All the Christians who have continued the tradition of blood sacrifice. A blood sacrifice that seems ineffectual in capturing the essence of Jesus' mission: "Love one another!" Please save Jesus. Take him down from the crucifix as his early Jewish followers once did. Allow him to be in glory. Take the heavy price tag off of his head, and he will be glorified.

Christianity tells us, the greatest act of love and sacrifice in the history of the world, is the conscious and willing acceptance by Jesus, of the brutality and suffering of crucifixion for our sins. If this is true, the greatest act of Christian love would be to free Jesus and save him from the everlasting stigma of Christianity.

THE IMMACULATE CONCEPTION

I have a personal connection to the Blessed Mother. I also have a deep connection with my mother, Saint Harriet. My birthday is on December 12. It is the feast of Our Lady of Guadalupe. The building I live in has a store in it, an Italian deli. I often walk out the front door and find coins on the ground. People drop them by mistake or don't want pennies in their pockets and throw them on the ground. On one particular day, I saw what appeared to be a dime laying in front of my door. I picked it up, and was surprised to find it was a medal of Our Lady of Guadalupe. Pretty amazing! A message from the Angels. I keep it close to my heart.

The Immaculate Conception Doctrine states: "Mary, through the merit of her son Jesus, was conceived without sin." The doctrine of the Immaculate Conception is essential, especially in the Catholic religion. Christianity teaches all humans are sinners, due to the original sin of Adam and Eve. We all need redemption. This redemption is ours through the sacrifice, death, and resurrection of Jesus. Here is a theological question. If Mary had been tainted by original sin, as all humans are, and she was the mother of Jesus, Jesus must also be tainted by original sin. Quite a dilemma for Christianity. Therefore, Mary became immaculately conceived. But then, would the sacrifice of Jesus redeem Mary? She was without sin. She did not need redemption. Christian Theologians did not agree on how to fix this tricky problem, and whether or not Mary needed redemption. Some Church fathers like Saint Thomas Aquinas, Saint Bonaventure, and Bernard of Clairvaux were not comfortable with the way the Church taught this doctrine. It took a Papal Apostolic constitution "Ineffabilis Deus" in 1854, by Pius IX to settle any disputes. They couldn't agree for almost 2000 years. The Scribes and Pharisees of the Church were acting at their best.

Jesus disrespected Mary, his mother, at times. Certainly, there were times I disrespected my mother. It is part of growing up and becoming an independent being. Jesus had a better excuse than I. He was doing the work of his Father in Heaven. He didn't want to be bothered with her request at the Wedding Feast at Cana. He denied her when he said, "Who is my mother?" (Matthew 12:48) He even rejects the concern of Mary and Joseph when he was in the Temple with the scholars. "And he said unto them, How is it that ye sought me? wist ye not that I must be about my Father's business?" (Luke 2:49) How does Mary deserve to be the elevated "Queen of Heaven?" Not that I would ever think of taking any title or office away from her. Surely, she suffered much from the personal disgrace of being pregnant and unwed, rejected, and then witnessing the rejection and crucifixion of her son.

Why is Mary, the Blessed Mother, so important? The Church needed to address the Divine Feminine. Approximately half of the people of the world are born female. The early Christian movement was, like the culture of the times, male-dominated. However, there has been a long tradition of female goddesses and heroines throughout the history of the many different cultures, societies, mythologies, and religions. Mary became the personification of the Divine Feminine for the Church. They needed to address the feminine principle of God, even if they never talked about it, respected it, or recognized it. It still manifested due to its inherent power.

What intrigues me most concerning the Blessed Mother is not her many titles, but her apparitions. In Fatima, the children report seeing a woman "brighter than the sun" She was holding a rosary. This apparition became known as "Our Lady of the Holy Rosary." In Lourdes, a petite woman appeared to Bernadette Soubirous. She said she was the Immaculate Conception. I already addressed the problems surrounding that title. In Egypt, she floated above St. Mark's Coptic Church. She was the Black Madonna as Our Lady of Czestochowa. In Japan, she spoke to a deaf nun through a statue. In Paris, she appeared sitting in a chair. In Knock, Ireland, she stood a few feet above the ground.

All of these apparitions are amazing, but I think the most interesting apparition is "Our Lady of Guadalupe." Here she appears as a native woman to speak to Juan Diego. She gave him roses in December (out of season) to give to the local bishop. They became the image on the miraculous Tilma (a fiber cloak). The point is this: she appears slightly or very different in each apparition. How can this be? What magic is this? Isn't she the same person? Her apparitions remind me of the appearances of Zeus. He changed his form when he appeared to humans. Could it be, the Divine Feminine is using the collective consciousness to bring a message of hope and healing? A message needed in Christianity. Just ponder this: At Fatima, "the Miracle of the Sun" occurred. Over 70,000 people reported seeing the sun dance in the sky. If the sun danced in the sky, people all over Europe would have reported this incredible phenomenon. But they did not!

SAINT HARRIET

Saints are special people in the eyes of Christianity. I know my mother was a saint in my eyes. She suffered much on the physical, emotional, and psychic levels, but she never gave up her faith. Near the end of her life, she developed diabetes. She had a leg amputated. What an addition to her suffering from Rheumatoid Arthritis for 50 years. During her decline, she came under the influence of born again Christians. They helped her and ministered to her, but they also perverted her love. I was living in Rochester, New York, at the time. I was practicing Psychic-Mediumship and healing as part of my religion, Spiritualism. I was also an Astrologer. She would call me and say, "Son, are you still doing the work of the devil?" She would ask this question with venom in her voice. I have been attacked, threatened, and experienced discrimination by Christians many times, because I am a Spiritualist Minister, Psychic Medium, and Astrologer. You get used to their fear and hatred. However, when your mother attacks you in this way, it can have a potent effect on you. She was slowly killing me. One time, I was so emotional, it led to a car accident. She called me about a week later and started on me again, "Son, are you still doing the work of the devil?" I know spirit put the answer in my mouth because the words just flew out without my thinking. "No mom, I'm not doing the work of the devil . . . I'm just a little horny!" (A friend had recently given me a Garfield doll dressed like the devil with horns.) She couldn't help herself, my words must have caught her completely off guard, and she laughed. As she laughed, I heard a loud snap in my mind, like snapping your fingers. I was free; my mother and her fear didn't own me anymore. This experience is one reason why I would like to see Jesus set free.

I told this story to a woman friend. Her comment was, "Wow; your mother was a real bitch!" Her strong reaction stopped me. I had never thought of my mother in that way, and I still don't today. I do think of her as a saint. The burdens she carried were extreme, but they did not deter her faith. I have studied the lives of Catholic Saints. Many of their challenges do not even come close to my mother's. Some were saints because they were popes, or did something for the Church. They might have given the Church money or land. They were not all people who lived an exceptional life. Some of them were not particularly friendly people. Most did not perform miracles. My mother, Saint Harriet, was amazing in her commitment and her love. I did not always agree with her, but she was an extraordinary being.

WWJD

I cringe every time I see an athlete make the sign of the cross after winning a game or making a score. He or she is thanking Jesus for his special blessing. Imagine, Jesus let this particular athlete defeat a foe. How about the losers? What if they're also Christian? Maybe they should have prayed harder for the blessing of winning. Did they sin, and lose the favor of Jesus?

The "What Would Jesus Do" signs people used to display at basketball or football games inspire a similar idea. They bring up an important question to ask at the end of this book. Would Jesus attend a football game at Notre Dame Stadium? I doubt it! He couldn't afford the ticket. Would Jesus praise the bureaucracy of the Church and Christians, who say they love God, but hate one another and others? How about the innumerable atrocities committed in his name? Would he be happy about them? No one, who has walked on this earth, has been more poorly represented than Jesus. But Jesus knew! He even addressed the issue with his dying words, "Then said Jesus, Father, forgive them; for they know not what they do." (Luke 23:34)

Thomas F. Kearns

CHAPTER 7 - WHO WILL FREE JESUS?

Imagine Living in a world without light and warmth. Prometheus stole fire from the Gods and gave it to humanity. Zeus punished him, but he was a hero for humanity. The light and heat of fire helped humankind grow and thrive. It freed us from reliance on the Gods. Zeus punished Prometheus by chaining him to a rock. An eagle (the symbol of Zeus) would devour his liver each day. It would grow back each night. This set in motion a cycle of eternal suffering. It took the hero Hercules to break the chains of Prometheus and set him free.

The New Testament tells us, the Jewish followers of Jesus took him down from the cross and buried him in the tomb. It gave him the opportunity to rise from the dead, ascend to heaven, and end his suffering. Unfortunately, the later Christians put the tortured, mutilated, and broken body of Jesus back on the cross, so he could suffer throughout eternity. His eternal suffering would be used to remind humanity of its guilt. Humanity has killed God!

The Hero Hercules freed Prometheus. Who will be the hero and free Jesus from eternal suffering, and humanity from eternal guilt?

There are only two possibilities.

Jesus can return in the promised Second Coming of the "Son of man." It would not only save him from further suffering but also free the human race. However, Jesus must be looking down from heaven, wondering if humankind is ready for the full glory. It does not appear that way.

Humankind can begin living what Jesus taught. "A new commandment I give unto you, That ye love one another; as I have loved you, that ye also love one another." (John 13:34) It would Free Jesus, and he would come again and bring all the glory of salvation.

Both are possibilities. But, it has been over 2000 years.

Thomas F. Kearns

Light from Water

Thomas F. Kearns

CHAPTER 8 - MANCHURCH

(An excerpt from The Art of the Mystic.)
Religion and spirituality are a serious universal phenomena. Both men and women seek to worship a deity or deities they can in no way comprehend. Each individual, at some point or another in life, must try to understand what religion and spirituality are all about and what they mean in their lives. One purpose of the Manchurch poster is to show the variety of ways people try to express their spiritual and religious understanding.

A spiritual or religious expression may seem to be the same, but in practice, they are often different. In my opinion, often very different. Religion tends to be a code, practice, and belief system that links people to God through a church. In simple terms, the church or people who run the church define this code and outline specific rules each member must follow regarding the way they live their life.

Many religions give you the feeling their members are made right in the sight of God by living the code. Churches are organizations, and they often lose sight of their original mission. In this case, to serve the people so they can be closer to God. Unfortunately, the people usually wind up serving the organization so it may perpetuate itself.

The act of acknowledging and worshiping God should be a natural spiritual expression. It should allow each person to bring the best of themselves to the experience. Each individual should reach out with their particular gifts and blessings.

Perhaps due to the incomprehensible nature of God, we have been taught God is an outside force. However, God is also an inside force. Many religions teach we have an eternal soul. In a sense, this makes us part of God. Is not the soul part of God? If we need to worship God, might not God also need to be praised?

As part of the great collective of humanity, each person shares many experiences with the whole. The experience of watching a beautiful sunset might be an individual experience to a person, but it is also an experience available to almost all and God. It is a humbling thought. God knows every sunset, every pebble on the beach, and every star in the night sky.

Religion has often created a prison in the minds of its followers. The adherents must follow a specific set of beliefs to be one with God. We can see how humanity abused that over the centuries. Perhaps we need freedom from God. Yes, we are told we are made in the image and likeness of God. However, isn't it more accurate to say, we have created the image of God in our likeness? To find God, we must grow to understand our essence. We must touch the very miracle of life inside our being.

We have seen good and evil in the world. We have all experienced joy and sorrow. All of these things are part of a fantastic experience we call life. This life presents us with many different opportunities. Hopefully, there is a purpose to all this. How are we to know? We cannot know God. God is infinite. We are not! So perhaps we should take a different view as expressed in the Manchurch poster. We should try to understand most religions use different symbols and concepts to reveal a way to comprehend their teachings. The reason is God is beyond comprehension. Therefore God is a construction of what can be understood or we have created God in the image and likeness of humanity.

Thomas F. Kearns

REFERENCES

1) Bible, King James Version, Public Domain, All Bible references

2) Fragments, Hermann Samuel Reimarus originally published as "Fragments by an Anonymous Writer" after the death of Reimarus by his friend Gotthold Ephraim Lessing as part of his Zur Geschichte und Literatur in 1774-1778

3) Aquarius, by the Fifth Dimension - First performance: March 1969
Lyricists: James Rado, Gerome Ragni
Composers: Galt MacDermot, James Rado, Gerome Ragni

4) Rodan - Initial release: December 26, 1956
Director: Ishir Honda
Producers: Tomoyuki Tanaka, Frank King

5) Pinocchio - Originally published: 1883
Author: Carlo Collodi
Illustrator: Enrico Mazzanti

6) Men in Black - Release date: July 2, 1997 (USA)
Director: Barry Sonnenfeld
Producers: Laurie MacDonald, Walter Parkespg

7) Sidney Omar, an American Astrologer
Sagittarius 1972 - Penguin Books

8) The Eighth House, Sex and Death and Dollars, by Marc Robertson
Published 1979
American Federation of Astrologers

9) The Art of the Mystic : The Master Course in Spiritual and Psychic Development. Published: 1985, Manchurch, Albany, NY

10) Religion as Art, An Interpretation, Thomas Martland
Published: 1981, State University of New York Press, Albany, NY

11) Grafton Peace Pagoda - Dedication 1993
Jun Yasuda, Buddhist Nun - Nipponzan Myohoji order

12) The Five Gospels - The Search For The Authentic Words Of Jesus - What Did Jesus Really Say? 1998 by Funk, Robert W.; Hoover, Roy W. and the Jesus Seminar - New Translation and Commentary

The Acts of Jesus: What Did Jesus Really Do? Apr 15, 1998 by Robert Walter Funk and The Jesus Seminar.

13) Jesus, Interrupted: Revealing the Hidden Contradictions in the Bible, by Bart D. Ehrman, Published: March 2009, HarperCollins

Misquoting Jesus' the Story Behind Who Changed the Bible and Why. by Bart D. Ehrman, Published: March 2005, HarperCollins

14) The Mythmaker, Paul and the Invention of Christianity by Hyam Maccoby

15) Fear and Trembling, by Soren Kierkegaard,
Originally published: October 16, 1843

16) The Prophet, by Kahlil Gibran
Originally published: 1923

17) The Birth of Christianity, John Dominic Crossan
Published: 1998, Harper Collins, New York

18) Fiddler on the Roof, 1964
Music, Jerry Bock; Lyrics, Sheldon Harnick; Book Joseph Stein

19) Basic Writings, by Martin Heidegger
Originally published: 1977

20) The Grand Inquisitor, a poem in Fyodor Dostoevsky's novel The Brothers Karamazov. Published: 1879

21) Myths, Dreams, and Mysteries: The Encounter Between Contemporary Faiths and Archaic Realities by Mircea Eliade Published: 1975 by Harper & Row (first published 1957)

22) The First Coming: How the Kingdom of God Became Christianity by Thomas Sheehan, Published: 1986 Random House

23) Man and His Symbols by Carl Jung
First published in 1964

24) The Hero with a Thousand Faces by Joseph Campbell.
Originally published: 1949, Princeton University Press

25) For Christ's Sake by Tom Harpur
Published 1986, Oxford University Press

Light from Water

www.ingramcontent.com/pod-product-compliance
Lightning Source LLC
Chambersburg PA
CBHW050559300426
44112CB00013B/1994